...just think about that!

OUTLINES FOR SECONDARY ASSEMBLIES

Compiled by Phil Wason

Scripture Union

© Scripture Union 1997

First published 1997

Scripture Union, 207-209 Queensway, Bletchley, Milton Keynes, MK2 2EB, England.

ISBN 1 85999 088 6

Permission to photocopy
Permission is given for teachers and those leading assemblies to photocopy illustrations only.

British Library Cataloguing-in-Publication Data. A catalogue record of this book is available from the British Library.

Design and illustration by Patricia Donnelly Graphic Design.

Printed and bound in Great Britain by Ebenezer Baylis & Son Limited, The Trinity Press, Worcester and London.

CONTENTS

ACKNOWLEDGEMENTS

I want to thank the following for their contributions which may have been adapted, altered or amalgamated:

Steve Bullock: *18 Soap*
Scott Carr: *25 Bring on the substitute!*
Wayne Dixon: *17 The most powerful thing in the world*
Gareth Evans: *1 The great crisp challenge*
Paul Fenton: *5 Why do they do that? and 37 Hidden meanings*
Andrew Gough: *27 In God's image and 13 Choices, choices*
Anita Haigh: *2 Understanding umbrellas*
Mark Reasbeck: *21 Identikit*
Andrew Smith: *31 It could be you!*
John Stephenson: *3 Walk in the light and 24 Trapped!*
David Wilkinson: *6 The kiss and 29 The universe, God and me*

Thanks also to:

Patrick Bamber, Julie Fleming, Julie Sharp and members of the Schools Ministry Network for inspiration and ideas; Leena Lane and 'Tricia Williams for editorial work; Christian Publicity Organisation, Worthing for *Hey!* used in *28 Best of friends* and 'Reasons why I never wash' used in *18 Soap,* with kind permission.

It has not been possible to trace the original sources of all the material in this book. Some of the material has appeared previously in:

Scripture Union in Schools publications (outlines 3, 10, 20, 26);
SALT, Scripture Union (outlines 1, 2, 4).

And other sources from which material has been adapted are:

Thinking clearly about God and Science, David Wilkinson and Rob Frost, Monarch (outline 6);
Hitting the Target, Chris Chesterton, Youth for Christ (outline 31).

To Annette, Fay and Dale

INTRODUCTION

This book is designed to equip you, the Christian visitor or teacher in school, with a range of assembly ideas so that you can take up the challenge of leading school worship and do so effectively and in a way that is acceptable to the school.

The 1988 Education Reform Act gives schools the legal responsibility to further the spiritual and moral development of young people. In addition to what Christians usually understand by the word 'worship', this can include helping pupils to examine their own beliefs, and to understand the significance of the Christian faith and its teaching.

In recent years, many new opportunities have opened up for Christians to help schools in this area. Before doing so, however, it is important to understand the legal and ethical framework we need to have in mind when working in schools.

Collective worship in schools:

THE 1988 EDUCATION REFORM ACT AND CIRCULAR 1/94

This act applies to maintained schools in England, and similar provisions apply in Wales. The provisions for Northern Ireland and Scotland are different in some respects (in Scotland, primary schools are only required to provide an act of worship once a week and secondary schools once a month), but similar in nature. However, the comments below which refer to the situation in England, should help you to focus on some of the considerations which lie behind what schools do. These comments refer to the law for county schools only. The law is different for church schools in that they have to conform to the trust deed of the school and will often be distinctly Christian.

The 1988 Education Reform Act requires that all pupils be involved in a 'daily act of collective worship which is wholly or mainly of a broadly Christian character'. Circular 1/94 was an attempt to explain the meaning of this. Unlike the Act, Circular 1/94 is advice and therefore not on the statute book. Their combined guidance is as follows:

- The terms 'assembly' and 'worship' are differentiated. An assembly is the time when the whole school or parts of the school, like year groups, are gathered together for notices and other administrative purposes and perhaps to foster the school 'ethos'. All staff and pupils are obliged to be present for this. The 'worship' element differs in that both staff and pupils have the right to opt out (or be withdrawn by parents, in the case of pupils).

- In practice, assembly and worship are put together into a single slot which we usually still call 'assembly'.

- Collective worship is not the same as corporate worship. The Education Reform Act implies, by using the term 'collective', that although the school community has gathered together to participate in an act of worship, they do not necessarily share the Christian faith. What unites them is the fact that they are part of the same school community, with pupils from backgrounds of no faith and other faiths.

- The majority of acts of worship 'must be wholly or mainly of a broadly Christian character'. This means that they should reflect the broad traditions of Christian belief, although they can contain material from non-Christian sources.

- Circular 1/94 says that collective worship should in some sense reflect something special and separate from ordinary school activities, being concerned with reverence or veneration paid to a divine being or power.

- School worship must not be distinctive of any particular denomination. It is not appropriate, therefore, to speak of the practices of one denomination as though they were the practices of all Christians.

- It should be appropriate to the ages, aptitudes and family backgrounds of all pupils, enabling all to take part.

- 'Taking part' in collective worship implies more than simply passive attendance. It should be capable of eliciting a response from pupils.

- The aims of collective worship in schools, according to Circular 1/94, are 'to provide the opportunity for pupils to worship God, to consider spiritual and moral issues and to explore their own beliefs; to encourage participation and response, whether through active involvement in the presentation of worship or through listening to and joining in the worship offered; and to develop community spirit, promote a common ethos and shared values and reinforce positive attitudes'.

A lot more could be said here on the subject of the law and collective worship in schools. However, it is important to remind ourselves that taking assemblies in school doesn't only have a legal dimension. We need to address ethical issues as well. It's helpful to think about how we would feel if a visitor of another faith was coming to take an assembly in our local school. What would we be happy (or unhappy) with them doing or saying? We then need to ask ourselves if we can work by the same code of conduct. This point will be developed in the next section ...

'Do's and 'don't's for visitors taking assemblies

APPROACHING THE SCHOOL

• Analyse your motives. Are you 'getting in'? Is this an opportunity for YOU? Are you recruiting for your church? It will show!
• Develop links with the school. Find other ways of helping the school, so that your taking assemblies becomes part of an on-going relationship.
• Write to the head, follow it up with a phone call and if possible an interview. It may be with a deputy or head of year. This is where you start to build relationships and establish credibility.
• Explore the possibilities of working together in partnership with other churches or organisations.
• Pray. This is God's work and his Spirit is always at work behind the scenes.
• Be patient. Teachers are busy. Don't get angry, but prayerfully and patiently persevere.

BEFORE THE ASSEMBLY

• Find out about the school. Where is it? How long will it take you to get there? Which entrance should you use?
• Observe an assembly, if possible, to get the 'feel' of the school. It will help you relax when it's your turn.
• Which room is it in? Don't assume it's the main hall. It could be in a sports hall or canteen!
• How long is the assembly? What is the age range? How many pupils will there be approximately? What else will be happening apart from your bit?
• Prepare thoroughly. Don't just expect to say 'something' about this or that. You will probably have between seven and ten minutes in a

secondary school, so you need to know exactly what you are going to say and how long each little bit will take.

- Try out any visual aids and find out where the power points are.
- Talk to the member of staff responsible for the assembly. Tell them about the kind of things you may do. This will help them to feel at ease about your visit.

THE ASSEMBLY

- Arrive with plenty of time to spare, so that you can 'set up' any props and feel relaxed, not rushed.
- What is the aim? What one point do you want to leave them thinking about?
- Content: is it interesting and relevant to the age group? It need not all be full of 'the Christian message'. You can make your point in less than a minute or with a question. You can challenge assumptions and beliefs in today's society as well as introducing pupils to the Christian faith.
- Never use Christian 'jargon' or assume any great previous knowledge of the Christian faith. Move from the familiar to the unfamiliar.
- Check that your props and visual aids will 'work' and be visible from the back of the hall.
- First impressions are very important in an assembly. A surprise element, a game, a question or just your opening words can set the tone for the whole assembly.
- Music and drama, done well, can be very powerful. Done badly, it can be a turn-off! Few secondary schools have singing as part of the assembly these days, except perhaps for Christmas. Drama must be punchy and well-rehearsed.
- Humour is an almost essential component, if it can be combined with, and not detract from, the main point – but nothing political, sexist or racist! It's not appropriate to refer to the graffiti you may have seen on the way in, or how you hated school when you were a teenager, or about the mental stability of all maths teachers! If you intend involving pupils or staff in the assembly, you should check your ideas out with a reliable source before!
- Timing: be short and snappy. Don't overrun. If possible, ask for notices etc to be given before your input.
- There is no need to be ultra formal in your appearance and in the way you dress, but you should be smart.
- Speak up so that everyone in the assembly can hear you, but not so that you are shouting all the time. Make use of opportunities to vary your tone and level of voice. Remember, *how* you say things can convey as much as *what* you say.
- It's good to refer to the Bible and even quote from it, but avoid

reading long passages, as this will lose pupils' attention.
• Ask, in advance, whether the assembly usually includes a prayer. If it does, pray. If it doesn't, you could conclude by asking a question which needs quiet reflection, or a moment's silence as an appropriate alternative.
• Are you preaching or educating? The assembly is part of the educational process in the school. The pupils would not necessarily choose to be present. As such, they are a captive audience. It is not your opportunity to 'preach the gospel', although you can tell them about it. It is not your opportunity to tell them what to do, although you can tell them what *you* have done. You can use expressions like: 'As a Christian, I believe ...' or, 'The message of the Christian faith is ...' – and still get your message across.
• Remember, the word 'worship' may well not be an appropriate one to use for the vast majority in the assembly hall. The nearest many young people may come to worship during the assembly will be an increased awareness, admiration or respect for Jesus or the Christian faith. You could think of taking an assembly as a kind of 'thought for the day' for young people.

AFTER THE ASSEMBLY

• Ask for feedback. Teachers (and pupils) can be most helpful. Ask a Christian pupil you know what their non-Christian friends thought about the assembly.
• If possible, spend a bit of time in the school, chatting with the head or deputy or any member of staff. All this is part of becoming a friend of the school.
• Have your diary with you so that you can arrange another couple of dates.
• Adapt – both yourself and the assembly. Look for ways to improve or update the presentation.
• Pray about ways in which the assembly might be followed up. Are there opportunities to build friendships with pupils and staff – through a Christian group, lessons or other school activities? Could your church be more involved?

The assembly outlines

Many of the assemblies in this book are 'interactive', that is, they require some participation on the part of pupils. This may simply be in the form of one or two volunteers helping you, for example, by attempting a task;

or it may involve more of a 'game show' approach, which sees you as the 'host' or 'compère'. It may take some practice and plenty of preparation, not to mention courage, to take this kind of assembly, but the rewards are an attentive 'audience' and therefore the opportunity to make a simple point to young people on the edge of their seats!

Other assemblies included are what you might call 'talks'. Memorise the content, so that you are free to concentrate on your presentation; use words and expressions that you are comfortable with. This kind of assembly may not require as much in the way of props or participation, but just as much prayer and preparation!

Both of these broad categories often require an OHP or large pieces of card or a flipchart to display words and pictures (make sure they are visible to all the audience). A game show with a name is so much more convincing! Display it on the screen. The name of the game or title of the assembly displayed for everyone to see serves as a reinforcement of the main point!

Each assembly outline has the following sections.

AIM

This is a summary of the main point of the assembly.

BIBLE BASE

Some outlines include a Bible base. Bible references given here are not necessarily intended to be used during the assembly. Sometimes they are simply there to help with your preparation before the assembly and indicate the biblical basis for the material.

YOU WILL NEED

This is a list of any props, OHP acetates, paper etc, that you will need in the assembly.

PREPARATION

This section tells you what you need to do beforehand. It may be the preparation of OHP acetates or charts or visual aids. Don't be put off or daunted! Thinking each step through carefully will help you enormously in your presentation of the assembly.

CONTENT

This contains the main substance of the assembly. You may be given quite detailed instructions on precisely what to do or say. That is because these are tried and tested assemblies, so you are following 'the maker's instructions'; but an assembly may work better for you if you tackle things slightly differently. Don't be afraid of adapting the contents of this book to suit your own situation and style. Adding your own anecdotes and examples will help to make the whole assembly more natural, more your own.

APPLICATION

This is usually a fairly brief part of the assembly. It's the part where you are trying to help the pupils make the link between the activity and entertaining aspects of the assembly and the spiritual or moral aim of the assembly. This could be done in little more than a moment, in a question or in suggesting that the pupils take some time to think quietly about what has just been said.

It's in this section that the pupils have the opporunity to 'respond'. Given all that has been said so far, here are some suggestions as to the nature of their response:

- It could simply be an increased awareness or understanding of an aspect of Christian truth.
- It could be a sense of awe and wonder.
- It could be a change in attitude towards something that had previously been discounted.
- It could be a moment's reflection on the meaning and purpose of life.
- It could be a determination to take some practical action to help others.
- It could be a desire to be different or better in some way.
- It could be a desire to find out more about what's been said during the assembly!

KNOW WHAT YOU BELIEVE

1 THE GREAT CRISP CHALLENGE

aim

To encourage pupils to consider Christianity for themselves, not just to believe what others tell them.

Bible base

Psalm 34:8 – taste and see that the Lord is good.

You will need:

- 6 different flavoured packets of crisps (choose a well-known brand with different coloured packets for different flavours)
- A 'Great Crisp Challenge' score-card (see illustration)
- A blindfold

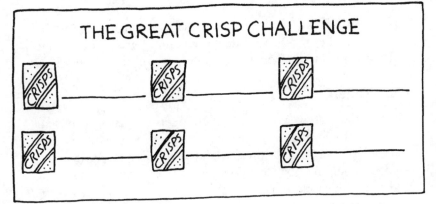

THE GREAT CRISP CHALLENGE

Preparation

- In advance, carefully open the bottom of the crisp packets and swap the contents of each packet with another one. Then carefully sellotape them back together.
- Prepare a 'Great Crisp Challenge' score-card, as illustrated, on card or OHP acetate. The contestants' verdicts on the flavour should be written in the spaces next to the pictures.

Content

1 Announce the 'Great Crisp Challenge'. Ask for a volunteer

who regards him/herself as a crisp expert.

2 Blindfold the volunteer and ask him/her to taste crisps from each packet, making sure the packet is opened at the top! Make sure the rest of the audience can see the packet. As your volunteer tests each packet, ask what flavour the crisps are.

3 As the verdict is given on each packet, the audience will be tempted to laugh or jeer as they see the volunteer seemingly getting it all wrong. Record the verdicts on the chart and encourage a round of applause as you take the blindfold off your volunteer.

4 Go through the answers and ask how the volunteer feels about his/her decisions.

5 Then reveal that some 'devious' person had switched the contents of the packets and that, actually, your volunteer has done remarkably well (even four out of six is very good scoring!).

6 Make the point that everyone else was judging simply by looking at the packaging, but the volunteer was the only one who was prepared to open it up and taste for him or herself.

Application

1 Say that this is typical of many people today. We buy or receive gifts in huge attractive boxes only to find vast amounts of polystyrene, a little present and a big disappointment. We judge people by how they look, what they wear and even the label on their clothing, without taking time to discover the person beneath.

2 For many, it's like that with Christianity, the Church, God, Jesus, the Bible. The Christian faith probably hasn't done a very good job of 'packaging' itself – but what lies beneath its image? Basing a decision just on how it looks won't give us an accurate answer. There's something more that we need to do – find out for ourselves.

3 A verse in the Bible says: 'Taste and see that the Lord is good' (Psalm 34:8, *New International Version*). Conclude by challenging the pupils not to judge anyone or anything simply by the outside appearance – including the Christian faith. They need to try it for themselves.

2 UNDERSTANDING UMBRELLAS!

aim

To challenge pupils to start reading the Bible for themselves.

Bible base

Jeremiah 29:11-13 – 'When you search for me ... you will find me.'

You will need:

- An assistant to help you with the sketch
- An umbrella
- A watering can half-filled with water
- A towel
- A modern version of the Bible – one with an attractive cover (eg *Youth Bible*, Nelson Word)

Preparation

- In advance learn and rehearse the sketch with your assistant. Your assistant should play the part of the shopper, while you play the parts of the narrator and the shopkeeper.
- It may be wise to ask permission about spraying water on the floor. Have a mop handy!

Content

The umbrella sketch

1 Start straight away with the umbrella sketch:

Narrator: A man walked into a shop and asked ...

Man: 'Scuse me, it looks like rain outside. Have you got an umbrella?

Shopkeeper: Yes Sir, I think so.

Narrator: So he gives the man the umbrella and the man goes outside ... *(At this point, pour water from the watering can over the man.)* ... and gets wet! So the man goes back into the shop ...

Man: 'Scuse me, I bought this umbrella here and I took it outside and I still got wet!

Narrator: The shopkeeper looks at the man, the umbrella and the audience, 'tuts' and says ...

17

Shopkeeper: You're supposed to put it over your head!

Man: O-o-h!

Narrator: So, the man went outside and put it over his head ... *(Pour water over him again)* ... and he still got wet! So the man went back into the shop.

Man: 'Scuse me, I bought this umbrella here, I took it outside, put it over my head and I still got wet!

Narrator: The shopkeeper looks at the man, the umbrella, the audience, 'tuts' and says ...

Shopkeeper: You're supposed to open it, Sir!

Man: O-o-oh!

Narrator: So, the man took the umbrella outside, opened it, and ... *(Pour water over the umbrella top)* ... he didn't get wet!

2 Round of applause!

Application

1 Say something like: 'How daft to have an umbrella and not open it ... not put it to the use for which it was intended!' Comment that that is exactly how many people treat the Bible. They judge it without opening it. It was never meant to gather dust on the shelf, it was meant to be opened and put to use!

2 Show the pupils a modern version of the Bible – one with an attractive cover. Comment that fortunately the packaging of the Bible has improved in recent years. Even so, the words inside are exactly the same and just as relevant as they always have been. Tell them you are going to read some words from the Bible which God spoke through a prophet called Jeremiah as an example: 'I have good plans for you, not plans to hurt you. I will give you a hope and a good future ... And when you search for me with all your heart you will find me' (Jeremiah 29:11-13, *Youth Bible*, Nelson Word).

3 Ask if there is a Bible in their house, or perhaps the New Testament they were given by the Gideons. Where is it? It may be propping the bed up, used as a door stop, or just gathering dust!

4 Challenge your audience to take the Bible off the shelf or out of the cupboard and put it to the use for which it was intended – open it and read it for all it's worth!

3 WALK IN THE LIGHT

aim

To challenge pupils not to be misled by only looking at the Christian faith from one point of view.

Bible base

John 8:12 – Jesus is the light of the world.

You will need:

- An OHP
- 3 OHP acetates prepared as illustrated:
  OHP 1 – a medical emergency (upper half); a novelty race (lower half)
  OHP 2 – a thief about to pounce (upper half); a person trying to warn of imminent danger (lower half)
  OHP 3 – someone waiting to be served at a bank (upper half); a bank robbery (lower half)
- 9 small bananas
- 3 blindfolds

Preparation

- Prepare OHP acetates as illustrated.

Content

Go bananas!

1 Ask for three volunteers who are hungry, like bananas and who don't mind the embarrassment of eating them in public.

2 Explain that the aim of the exercise is to see who can eat three bananas in the shortest time. To help them concentrate, they will be blindfolded. Ask them to sit down and blindfold them.

3 Ask the audience to keep cheering the competitors – whatever happens – while they are eating!

4 On the command, 'Go!' the volunteers are to start eating. Then take the blindfolds off two of the volunteers. Indicate that you want them to stop eating but to keep quiet about what

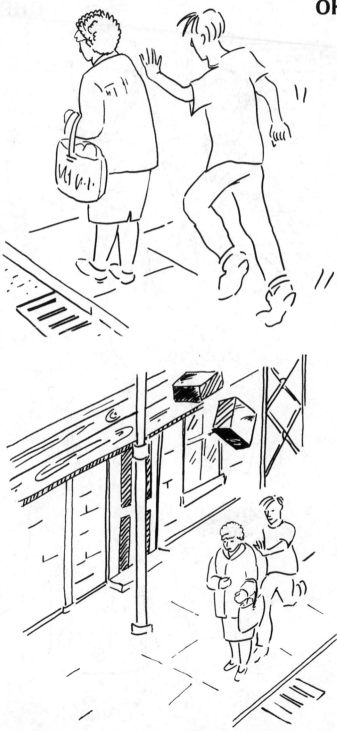

is happening. At the same time, encourage the audience to keep cheering, as they watch the lone performer stuffing bananas into his/her mouth! After a minute, bring the cruelty to an end, by declaring that you have a winner.

5 Take the blindfold off the lone competitor and watch for his/her reaction when they realise what has happened. Ask everyone to give the banana eater an extra big cheer and, as a prize, he/she wins – the other bananas!

In the dark?

1 Say how easy it is to be taken in when you've got a blindfold on. You can't be sure of what's happening! It's a bit like trying to find your way around a strange room, in the middle of the night, with no lights on! It's easy to stub your toe or stand on something. Then say that it's not only when we're in the dark that we can be confused ...

2 Display the scenes on the upper sections of the three OHPs, one after another. Ask the pupils what they see (a medical emergency; a thief about to pounce; someone at a bank).

Then display the three OHPs again, this time showing the scenes on the lower sections. Once more ask the pupils what they see (a novelty run in a race; a warning about imminent danger; a bank robbery).

3 Point out that none of them was wearing a blindfold and the lights were on, but they were still taken in.

Application

1 Ask pupils if they think it is possible to go through life as though they were wearing a blindfold. The Bible makes it clear that it is, especially when it comes to thinking about what is right and wrong, or about God. In fact, the Bible suggests that not looking at life from God's point of view is like constantly going around in the dark!

2 Jesus made an amazing claim when he said: 'I am the world's Light. No one who follows me stumbles around in the darkness. I provide plenty of light to live in'* (John 8:12).

He wasn't meaning that we can't actually see without him, but that we may not be fully aware of what's happening before

---

* This quotation is taken from *The Message*, Eugene Peterson, NavPress.

our very eyes, because we are only looking at things from one point of view – or maybe because that's all we've ever been told.
3 Say that it's easy to be taken in if we only view things from one angle – especially if we leave God out. Doing that can lead to major errors of judgment on our part. Ask pupils if there are any ways in which they are likely to be taken in by only looking at, or listening to, one point of view (especially when they think about God, the church, the Bible etc).
4 Challenge them to be determined always to investigate, so that they can look at the whole picture.

4 TRUE OR FALSE?

aim

To help pupils understand that Christianity is a reasonable faith, but the only way to be convinced is to try it for yourself.

Bible base

John 14:6 – Jesus is the way, the truth and the life.

You will need:

- 3 sets of 'T' (for true) and 'F' (for false) cards
- A small prize for the winner of the 'True or false?' game

Content

True or false?

1 Ask for three volunteers and give each a set of 'T' and 'F' cards.
2 Explain that you are going to make a series of statements. You want the volunteers to help you decide whether these are true or false. As you make each statement you would like them to raise either their 'T' card or 'F' card to show whether they think it's true or false. They can keep their own score.
3 You could use the statements below or devise your own.
  • The greeting 'Yo!' comes from the Chinese word for 'peace'. *(False)*

- Attila the Hun, whose armies invaded large areas of Europe, was only 3'4" tall (1.02m). *(True)*
- Henry VIII's second wife, Anne Boleyn, had six fingers on one hand. *(True)*
- After Sir Walter Raleigh's death, his widow took his embalmed head with her wherever she went. *(True)*
- Mozart was the composer of 'Twinkle Twinkle Little Star'. *(True* – when he was five!)
- When King Ethelred was buried in 1016, he was found to be a woman. *(False)*

4 Ask what the scores are, award a prize to the winner and encourage a round of applause.

Talk about

1 Say that sometimes it's hard to know whether something is true or not. Sometimes you just know, because you've heard it before or been told, but sometimes what you thought was false actually turns out to be true. What you thought was fiction turns out to be fact! What you thought was a waste of time turns out to be the best thing since the Multimedia PC! For example:

- In 1962 the Beatles were told by the Decca Recording Company that groups playing guitars were on the way out. They were wrong!
- A scientist called Simon Newcomb said that flight by machines heavier than air was impossible, just eighteen months before the Wright brothers proved him wrong!
- The genius Albert Einstein was told by his teacher in Munich that he would never amount to much!

People can make huge errors of judgment sometimes, even when they really believe what they are saying is true. Perhaps we need to be more open-minded!

2 Then there are areas of life which are very difficult to prove true or false! For example:

- Liverpool (or other successful, popular team) are the best football team in Britain.
- Elizabeth I was a good queen.
- Fat is bad for the arteries.
- Communism does not work.
- My wife/husband loves me.

3 You may believe all of these to be true, but they are hard to prove. However, there is plenty of evidence to help you come to a verdict which you can also show others. For example:

• You could collect details of Liverpool's playing record over the past thirty years in league and cup matches in Britain and Europe, and make out a case!

• A married man could point to the fact that his wife shares her life with him, sometimes makes his food and washes his clothes, goes home and gets into bed with him! It's not proof, but these are strong indications as to how she feels about him!

Application

1 Explain that statements like 'God exists' come into this category. In order to prove his existence you would have to capture the Lord of all creation and put him in a box so that everyone could see him! Comment that there would be no sense of awe or mystery or faith in this. God would then be just like any other man-made god. In fact, he would cease to be God!

2 Continue by saying that you could discuss the question of the need for an origin or source of everything. Where did this world come from? Who was the designer, maker, 'first mover' of it all? How can something be produced out of nothing? Who made Adam and Eve? Who was responsible for the Big Bang? Where did the original matter or cosmic dust come from? These are all questions that demand an answer ... and the answer may be ... God! But even if you were *almost* persuaded, God's existence still couldn't be *proved* to be true.

3 People have discovered that the truth of God needs to be experienced. Christianity is a reasonable faith. There are lots of reasons to suggest that the existence of God is very *likely*, but the conviction that it is *true* comes from having met him through a faith in the man called Jesus Christ ... God, in human form.

4 Conclude with Jesus' words: 'I am the way and the truth and the life; no one comes to the Father except through me' (John 14:6, *New International Version*).

5 WHY DO THEY DO THAT?

aim

To encourage pupils to ask themselves why they do or don't believe in God.

Preparation

• This assembly idea is intended as a talk outline. Memorise the content, using words and expressions which you are comfortable with.

• Rehearse your presentation.

Content

Why do they do that?

1 Begin by saying that many of them will have seen the BBC programme *How do they do that?* which explores some of the mysteries of our modern society.

2 Say that in this assembly you are going to be asking the question, '*Why* do they do that?' Ask pupils to think about why people do some of the crazy things they do ... things that just can't be explained. For example:

• Why do people who go to the theatre put their best clothes on, only to sit in the dark for three hours?

• Why do people look out of the window on the tube train?

• Why do kamikaze pilots – the ones that destroy themselves and their planes by flying into enemy aircraft carriers – wear crash helmets?

• Why, when you're giving directions to someone over the phone, do you use hand signals?

3 Then give some examples of the silly things people say. For example:

• When drivers are waiting at traffic lights, why do they say, 'Come on, come on'?

• Why, when people have written to someone who's moved, do they write: 'I hope I got the address right'?

• When people are showing someone round the house they're selling, why do they say, ' ... And this is the bathroom'?

Why do people believe in God?

1 Say that the question you especially want to ask this morning (this afternoon etc) is, *why* do people insist on saying, 'I believe in God'? Why do they do that?

2 In one survey of 13,000 year 9 and 10 pupils, nearly 40% of them said they believed in God and 35% said they weren't sure, leaving only 26% who said they didn't believe! Why? Why do people believe that? Continue by talking about the alternatives:

THE ATHEIST

People who say there is no God are called atheists. Being an atheist means taking a huge step of faith. After all, atheists have to live with the constant threat of being proved wrong, even if it's not until after they die! It could be a risky business. Whereas if 'believers' are wrong, they still have all the advantages of a fulfilled life here on earth, in the misguided hope that there is a God, and will never be proved wrong – because if they are wrong, and there is no God, they'll simply pass into oblivion with everyone else.

THE AGNOSTIC

The people who say 'I'm not sure' are called agnostics. It's OK to be an agnostic, as long as you don't sit on the fence for too long. Because after all, if you think about it, either there is a God or there isn't! The agnostic will always be proved wrong. Someone said that being an agnostic is a bit like the Mersey Tunnel (use an example the pupils will be familiar with); it's OK to travel through, but you wouldn't like to live there!

THE BELIEVER

39% of people in the survey said, 'I believe in God'. That's a big proportion of the people sitting in this assembly. Maybe a lot of people say they believe in God, but aren't sure why. Here are a few reasons for believing in God, even though he can't be proved scientifically:

- **Creation.** Most people, despite the popular scientific theories, still end up saying, 'Yes, but what or who started it all in the first place? It's so beautiful, so ... designed. Who is the designer?'

• **The Bible.** It's in most homes, but hardly ever opened. Yet when someone who really wants to find out about God actually opens the Bible and reads about him, they find something strange happens ... It starts to make sense, especially when they read about the third reason for believing.

• **Jesus.** You just can't ignore this character. Most people say he was a good man, perhaps the best man that ever lived, and yet he said he'd come from God, that he was God – strange claims for such a good man to make. Was he lying? Did he really prove what he claimed by rising from the dead?

• **The church.** Despite all its difficulties and persecutions, the church has survived and keeps on growing. Tens of thousands of people turn to God every day. The problem is, as well as being the best advert for believing in God, the church can also be the worst advert. So the next reason for believing is often the decisive one.

• **Experience.** You usually find that people who are sure of God talk about him like a person they have met and know. Often they are people who started off by praying, 'God, I'm not even sure if you're there, but if you are ... ,' and then ended up becoming firm believers. They took a simple step of faith.

Application

1 Ask pupils why it is that people make their mind up about God, without really stopping to think? Why do they do that?
2 Challenge pupils to stop and think about him now.

6 THE KISS

You will need:

> **aim**
>
> To help pupils understand that science and the Christian faith are compatible.

- An OHP
- 4 OHP acetates prepared in advance as follows:

  OHP 1 – a picture of the famous sculpture 'The Kiss' by Rodin (sources: an art shop; your local library; alternatively, you could use any suitable picture of a kiss that can be copied onto OHP acetate)

  OHP 2 – quotation from Professor Paul Davies (see **Application** below)

  OHP 3 – quotation from Stephen Hawking (see **Application** below)

  OHP 4 – quotation from Genesis 1:1 (see **Application** below)

Preparation

- Prepare the OHP acetates as described.
- This assembly idea is intended as a talk outline. Memorise the content and rehearse your presentation carefully.

Content

Has science disproved the Bible?

Begin by asking pupils if they have ever heard it said that science has disproved God? Even 200 years ago, someone called Laplace told Napoleon Bonaparte that as far as God's role in science was concerned, he had 'no need for that hypothesis'. Today, some say, 'We now know that the universe comes from the Big Bang about 15 billion years ago, but the Bible doesn't mention anything about it. So therefore, science has disproved the Bible.'

Of course, it's true that the Bible talks about the universe being the creation of God. But do you have to make a choice between the Bible and science? Is one right and the other wrong?

Two ways of looking at things

Comment that we know in everyday life, it is possible to have two different descriptions of the same thing which are different but both true. For example:

- A scientist might say that playing the violin was rubbing the entrails of a dead sheep with the hairs of a dead horse! That description would describe the facts accurately, but it wouldn't answer all our questions – like why certain sounds were nice and others not so nice; or why violin music was enjoyable; or why the person was playing the violin in the first place!

• Here's another example. In answer to the question, 'Why is the grass burning?' the scientist might talk about the presence of oxygen, the combustible nature of grass and wind factors. But a vital part of the answer could also be a discarded cigarette, or the clearing of land, or whatever it was that triggered the fire in the first place.

'How?' and 'Why?' questions

1 Say that, in general, it's useful to think of science asking and trying to answer the 'How?' questions, and the Christian faith trying to tackle the 'Why?' questions. Science is about *mechanisms* (how did the universe come about?); the Bible talks about *meanings* (why did the universe come about?). There are many different kinds of books and God chose not to write a science textbook!

2 Talk about the following examples to help pupils think about the difference between the 'How?' and the 'Why?' questions:

• In answer to the question, 'Why did the man fall from the roof?' we could talk scientifically about the weight of the man, the slope of the roof, the pull of gravity and so on. Or we could talk about whether he slipped or was pushed or – did he jump? These are non-scientific questions. Gravity did not *make* the man fall!

Science has been brilliant at showing us *how* things work but sometimes has not been able to help us understand *why* they are there in the first place!

• An example from 'everyday life' – the kiss! **(Display OHP 1.)** What is a kiss? A kiss is the approach of two pairs of lips and the reciprocal transmission of carbon dioxide and microbes and the juxtaposition of two orbicular muscles in a state of contraction. That is a kiss ... explained scientifically!

But if you were to go up to a loved one and say, 'Darling, would you like to have a reciprocal transmission of carbon dioxide and microbes? And can I juxtapose my orbicular muscle in a state of contraction with yours?' the person might reply, 'Get lost!'

Of course most of us would describe a kiss quite differently: in terms of meaning and purpose and love and ... passion! (You might like to dramatise this bit!) This is quite different from the scientific description. But which is true?

In fact, both of them are true – but different. I suppose you could say that to have an accurate understanding of a kiss, you need both descriptions.

Application

1 Say that we perhaps shouldn't worry too much, therefore, if the scientific description of how the universe came into being is different from the Bible's claim that the universe is here because God created it.

2 Many of the people who made the first great steps in science were Christians, and many scientists today are again returning to talk in terms of something bigger than even they can comprehend. Maybe that's because we now see that science has not been the great solution to all human problems that people once hoped it would be. Maybe it's because we now understand that science can be our servant *or* our master; and maybe it's because the more that's discovered about our universe, the more we are in awe of its order and beauty.

3 Give these two examples of what scientists have said:
- Professor Paul Davies, who certainly wouldn't call himself a Christian believer, has said **(display OHP 2)**, 'Through my scientific work, I have come to believe more and more strongly that the physical universe is put together with an ingenuity so astounding that I cannot accept it as mere brute fact.'
- The celebrated Stephen Hawking, although not a Christian, acknowledges that if we knew all the answers to the 'Why?' questions, it would be the ultimate triumph of human reason, because then, he has said **(display OHP 3)**, 'We would know the mind of God.'

So, amongst scientists there is an increasing recognition that there are some things we will never fully understand, because we are not the creator.

4 Conclude by focussing pupils' attention on some words in the Bible, from the book of Genesis – the book of beginnings, which simply say **(display OHP 4)**: 'In the beginning ... God created the universe' (Genesis 1:1, *Good News Bible*).

7 THE ULTIMATE FEAR

Note: Check in advance with the school whether there have been any recent bereavements amongst the pupils, and whether they consider it is appropriate for you to talk about the topic of death in assembly.

aim
To help pupils to consider death and what lies beyond it.

Bible base
John 11:25 - life after death.

You will need:

- A matchbox containing a chocolate

Content

Introduction

1 Hold up the matchbox containing the chocolate and ask, 'Would you like to see what I've got in this box?' Ask pupils what they think might be in the box and whether they think they would like you to put whatever it is in their hand! Play along with any fears they might have – perhaps that it's a spider ... or something worse!

2 Eventually, choose one pupil to come to the front. Ask them to say what they think is in the box, before melodramatically reaching into the box and placing on their hand ... a chocolate!

3 Say that you expect that some people thought it was going to be a spider! Comment that we often fear the worst.

What frightens you?

1 Ask pupils what frightens them. Spiders? Heights? Confined spaces? Rats? The fear of being lost? Talk about one of the things that really frightens *you*. Explain that sometimes our fears are irrational – then they are called phobias.

2 In a recent survey of 14 – 16 year olds, 'death' came at or near the top of the list of their fears. Perhaps that's because they have been struck by the suddenness of death, for example, through taking the drug Ecstacy. Or maybe they have been frightened by a story, like the one in the news some time ago: a lady who had apparently 'died' at home was taken to the mortuary where the attendant spotted her breathing! He even said he had heard her snore! (Use these or other current

examples in the news.)

3 Comment that when we stop to think about it, most of us are frightened of death.

Why? Maybe it's because it's an event that we have no control over; it's final; it's stepping into the unknown; it could happen anytime. And anyway, you are enjoying life, you don't want to die! Woody Allen once said, 'I'm not afraid to die, I just don't want to be there when it happens!'

Talk about 'death'

1 Whether we like it or not, we are all going to die. It's been statistically proven that 100% of us will die. We have a one in one chance of dying!

2 People try to put it off as long as possible. One very rich American, Miller Quarles, has offered vast sums of money to anyone who can come up with something to help him live longer! And some people talk of having their bodies frozen in suspended animation until a super remedy for age and death is invented.

3 Somehow, although we're not taken in by these things, we avoid thinking or talking about the subject of death. It's a 'taboo' subject. It used to be sex that was the taboo topic. Now everyone talks about that and no one wants to talk about death. So we use other phrases for it, like 'at rest', 'passed away', 'fallen asleep', 'gone to meet his maker', 'kicked the bucket', 'snuffed it', 'tipped his clogs' and so on. So although we know it's coming, death still takes us by surprise.

4 Tell the story of 'Uncle George', who was part of a well-to-do, respectable American family. Unfortunately, he got in with the wrong crowd, became a gangster and eventually was convicted of shooting and killing someone, much to the shame of his family and was sentenced to death in the electric chair.

When it came to the question of what to write on his gravestone, his family said, 'We can't just write: "Here lies Uncle George – he got the chair"! We need something more respectable.' This is what they eventually decided to write on his gravestone: 'Here lies Uncle George. He held a significant seat in applied electronics at a major government institution. He was attached to his position with very strong ties and his death came as a great shock.' Absolutely true, but meaningless!

5 Explain that in years gone by, people were much closer to death. Often, the body would be kept in the house for several days, so that people could pay their last respects.

Nowadays, people live much longer, they are more likely die in hospital and we are separated from the event of death.

6 For many people, it's the death of a loved one that starts them thinking about God and about what happens when you die. Ultimately, it is what you believe about death that determines what you do with your life.

Is there life after death?

1 Announce that you are going to do a simple survey. Ask the front row of pupils in the assembly to stand and ask them: 'Is there life after death?' If they think the answer is 'no', they should go to the right of the assembly hall. If they think the answer is 'yes', they should go to the left. If they are not sure, they should go to the middle. Tell them that you want them to be completely honest.

2 When the 'survey' is complete, thank those involved and ask one or two people what made them stand where they did. Ask those who said 'no' or 'not sure', what it would take to convince them of life beyond death. They might talk about proof, like someone coming back from the dead, as being the necessary evidence.

Application

1 Explain that Christians' belief in life after death is based on what Jesus said and did. For example, on one occasion, he made this amazing claim. He said, 'I am the resurrection and the life. He who believes in me will live, even though he dies' (John 11:25, *New International Version*). As if to prove it, he then raised his friend Lazarus from the dead; and he himself rose on the third day after his crucifixion – something that was witnessed by at least 500 people.

2 Christians have discovered that the more they examine the evidence and the uniqueness of Jesus, the more they are led to the conclusion that – although death itself might be horrible – it is possible to have peace about what lies beyond it.

3 Conclude by reminding pupils of what you said earlier: what you believe about death determines what you do with your life.

SEEING IS BELIEVING?

aim

To challenge pupils' assumptions about contradictions in the Bible.

You will need:

- Objects arranged on a tray for the 'observation tray' game
- Pens and paper for the game participants
- A list of the objects being observed written on an OHP acetate or large piece of card
- An assistant (with 'unusual clothes' and 'strange mannerisms') who will enter during the assembly unannounced
- A briefcase
- A prize

Content

Note: When you take your place in front of the audience ready to begin the assembly, remember to put your 'briefcase' down beside you where it is clearly visible to all the pupils.

Observation test

1 Invite two or three volunteers to take part in a game of observation. Give them fifteen seconds to look at the objects on the tray and then remove it from sight.

2 Give each volunteer a pen and some paper and ask them to write down what they saw.

3 Meanwhile, comment to the audience that being observant is a very difficult thing. Illustrate this by telling the following funny anecdote:

- One day a snail was mugged by three slugs. He went to the police station and they said, 'Can you give us a detailed description?' He said, 'Oh, I don't know, it all happened so quickly!'

Make the point that the game participants don't have such an easy task as it might first appear!

4 Still whilst the volunteers are writing down what they remember, ask the pupils what it is that contains sixty-six books,

can be found in 2000 languages, was written by about forty authors and is the world's best seller? If no one comes up with the answer, tell them: the Bible! Explain that although it's the world's best seller, and most homes represented in the audience probably contain one, it is also hardly ever read by the majority of people in this country.

5 Turn back to the 'observation tray' game. Say that it's time to see how the contestants have got on. Display the list of objects. Give the volunteers a few moments to see how many they remembered. Give the winner a prize and encourage a round of applause for all the game participants.

The Bible

1 Explain that the Bible is the world's best selling book, but often, the least read – an amazing fact, considering that it is believed to be such a powerful a book that in some countries it is banned, even today.

2 People risk their lives in these countries by owning one; and others by smuggling them in. Only 500 years ago in Europe, it was an offence punishable by death to translate the Bible into a language that people could understand!

3 It's a book that has changed the lives of millions of people and shaped whole cultures. So it's amazing that so few people actually bother to find out what's in it! Maybe that's because:

- we forget that it's not so much a single book, as a library of books. You don't need to start at page one and read all the way through it, just as you wouldn't start at one end of a shelf of books and read to the other end!
- some people feel that you can't trust the Bible: it's so old now, the world's changed and anyway, there are lots of contradictions in it.

Reliable witnesses

1 At this point, your assistant, who has been hidden outside the room, should burst in, wearing some unusual clothing, saying something to some of the pupils on his way in. He then takes your briefcase and leaves. The 'thief' should reveal his face to some but not others in the room.

2 Act as though you are horrified. Say that the briefcase contained lots of money – but it's OK, because there are lots of

eye witnesses present who can give an account of what happened.
3 Ask three or four people from different parts of the room to say what they saw. Repeat what they say so that everyone can hear. There will be some information that only some people have.
4 Thank those who have spoken for being such reliable witnesses. Say that you have certainly got plenty of information to hand over to the police.
5 Then comment how interesting it is that if you all had to write down an account of what just happened, you would all write different things. Say that that's understandable because it happened so quickly. But you are sure they would all be telling the truth! It's just that they saw the events from different perspectives.

Contradictions in the Bible?
1 Continue by talking about the differences in the accounts of events in the Bible. For example:
   • In the Bible, one gospel says that Jesus healed two blind men, but in another gospel it only mentions one (Matthew 20:29–34; Mark 10:46–52).
   • One account of Jesus' entry into Jerusalem on a donkey, surrounded by thousands of people, also mentions the foal of the donkey. Another doesn't (Matthew 21:1–7: Mark 11:1–7).
2 But perhaps, as you have just had demonstrated with the incident of the 'thief', these differences in the accounts are understandable: there were many people around; there was so much going on; how someone describes an event depends on where they were and what they saw.
3 Those who took part in the observation game earlier, proved that even moments after an event, we struggle to remember small details. But everyone can agree about the main event, and that's what really matters.
4 In fact the slight differences in the gospel stories give a sense of authenticity. After all, if it was all made up by fanatics, you would expect stories that matched exactly. As it is, the gospels of Matthew, Mark, Luke and John – the four accounts of Jesus' life – actually complement one another.

Application
1 Those who talk about the Bible's contradictions often can't

produce any – probably because they haven't read it! The best way to discover for yourself the contents of this dynamic book, is to read it yourself. Challenge pupils to do just that, perhaps starting with one of the gospels – Matthew, Mark, Luke or John.

2 The Bible is full of great stories and will help you to find out about the man called Jesus. It claims to be a great instruction manual for every area of people's lives. And it claims to be reliable – the events it describes written down by people who were recording the amazing things they had actually seen and heard.

3 Conclude by saying that the Bible really can change people's lives.

9 FRIDAY 13TH

aim

To show pupils that what you believe in shapes your life; so it's important that what you base your life on is true and worthwhile

You will need:

- An OHP
- OHP acetates with pictures which illustrate a variety of superstitions about objects, events etc which people believe are 'lucky' or 'unlucky' (eg a four leaf clover; 'fingers crossed'; one magpie; walking under a ladder); and an acetate showing a list of the various superstitions you are going to refer to in the assembly.

Preparation

- Prepare the OHP acetates as suggested above.
- This assembly idea is intended as a talk outline. Memorise the content, using words and expressions you are comfortable with.

Content

Introduction

1 Begin by asking the pupils whether they knew that there are only ever one or two Friday 13ths in any school year (maybe this is one of them).

2 Friday 13th is meant to be a very unlucky day. Of course, this is just superstition and nobody believes in it really – or do they? Many people avoid planning a special event to happen on this day (eg getting married, flying).

Lucky or unlucky?

1 Explain that Friday 13th is just one example of something which is meant to be unlucky. There are plenty of other superstitions – which people believe bring them bad luck or good luck – which may affect their lives in some way.

2 Talk about some of the following superstitions, giving suggestions as to how they might have originated and illustrating some with pictures, speech balloons etc on OHP acetates.

- The four leaf clover.
- Throwing salt over your shoulder when cooking or eating. This is meant to scare off the devil who may have been

following you.
• Saying, 'God bless you!' when someone sneezes. This was once thought to ward off any evil spirits you may have breathed in!
• Saying, 'Touch wood!' or 'Fingers crossed!'. Both of these sayings probably originated in the idea of trusting in the cross that Jesus died on, and were therefore meant to bring the speaker good luck.
• Black cats. These were probably thought to be unlucky because of their association with witches. Also at night you can only see their eyes – which look sinister.
• Seven years' bad luck when you break a mirror. There were probably economic reasons for this superstition. The backs of mirrors used to be silvered with real silver and it would take seven years to save up the money to pay for it!
• Seeing a magpie on its own ('One for sorrow, two for joy'). Perhaps this was thought to be bad luck because it is a rare occurence, and so maybe was linked with other unusual events. Some people actually salute a lone magpie if they see one, for good luck.
• Don't pass on the stairs. Probably regarded as unlucky because of the danger of falling down.
• Don't walk under a ladder. Unlucky because you might get covered in paint or things might fall on you.
• Don't put your shoes on the table.
• Don't open an umbrella inside the house.
• If you pull a face, it will stay like that if the wind changes.

3 Display the OHP acetate showing the list of the different superstitions you have talked about. Referring to the list, comment that all of these examples are meant to bring bad or good luck. Then ask whether any of these things are really worth believing or trusting in. In fact, they are really just a mixture of superstition, common sense, old wives' tales, economics, pagan and Christian beliefs. Put them all together and you've got something which could be called 'folk religion'. Superstitions don't really have any power to bring you good or bad luck.

4 Say that many people, even though they wouldn't call themselves religious, try to make sense of life and find security by 'believing' in some of these superstitions. To do so means – as in the major religions – that they have to exercise a certain amount of faith.

5   In this country, many people are turning their back on materialism – the western dream. They feel that the 'system' has failed them – and maybe the church is part of that. So they are turning to New Age religions and a whole new alternative spirituality has become big business: folk religion and superstitions – some verging on the occult: horoscopes with millions of people reading theirs every day; faith in crystals or tarot cards.

Friday 13th

1   Explain that Friday 13th possibly came to be thought of as unlucky because of Jesus' death on Easter Friday.

2   Ask pupils why they think Christians call the day on which Jesus died '*Good* Friday'. Explain that although the crucifixion of Jesus was a terrible event, it meant that human beings could be friends with God because, in dying, Jesus had taken the punishment for our wrongdoing – and that's *good* news! Jesus knew the events on that Friday were going to happen. In fact he predicted them and believed they were the reason for his coming. And Jesus' death on the cross isn't just superstition – it's true.

Application

1   On a global scale, thousands of people put their faith in Jesus every day. Today, in Africa alone 15 – 20,000 people will turn to faith in Jesus Christ. Belief in Jesus affects the way people live and may mean radical change. But Christians believe it's worth basing your life on Jesus and his teachings, because what they know about him is based on truth and makes sense.

2   Ask pupils to think about the fact that everyone believes in something. Challenge them to ask themselves what they believe in and are basing their lives on. Explain that what you believe affects the way you treat yourself, treat others and view the world, the universe and beyond. What you believe shapes your hopes and dreams for the future. So it's important that what you believe in is true and worthwhile.

3   Conclude by saying that what you believe in determines what you think of a day like Friday 13th.

Note: This assembly outline could be used at Easter, as well as – of course – on a Friday 13th.

KNOW HOW TO LIVE

10 RIGHT OR WRONG?

Note: This assembly is particularly suitable for use with upper school pupils.

aim

To help pupils think about how they know what is right and what is wrong.

You will need:

- 20-30 sets of cards, each consisting of: 1 red, 1 green and 1 yellow card

Preparation

- Make the cards. (You could cut A4 coloured paper into 4 pieces.)
- Before the assembly begins, leave one set of cards on each seat of the front row of the assembly hall.
- In advance, prepare the list of situations for the 'right or wrong?' survey. (See suggestions below.)

Content

Introduction

1 Ask the pupils how they know what is right and what is wrong.

2 Comment that it's not easy to find a straightforward answer to this question today. To whom can you go to find an answer? Parents or teachers? Politicians or royalty? The church or celebrities?

Right or wrong? – a survey

1 Explain that this morning (this afternoon), you are going to ask some of them what *they* think, by using a simple survey.

2 Ask the pupils on the front row to pick up their cards.

3 Announce that you are going to read out some situations which have a moral dimension. After each one, you would like the people in the front row to raise one of the cards depending

on whether they think the situation is right (green card), wrong (red card), or neither right nor wrong (yellow card). Diffuse any potential embarrassment by assuring them that, as they are sitting on the front row, the rest of the audience will only see their raised card.

4 Read out a list of situations, which could include:
- a terrorist bombing;
- killing animals for their meat;
- shops opening on Sundays;
- leaving your wife or husband for someone else;
- spending all your time, energy and devotion on someone or something other than God;
- doing only what would make your family proud of you;
- claiming more insurance money than you should when you've been burgled;
- taking drugs;
- wanting all the things your friends have got.

For each situation (you could have more), the pupils raise the coloured card of their choice.

5 At the end, thank them all for taking part in the survey and for their honesty.

The moral maze
1 Comment that you could analyse the variety of results in the survey, but that what interests you most are *the reasons why* people have responded in the way they did. What do people base their answers on?

2 In the survey there was quite a spread of opinion on one or two of the issues and a lot of agreement on others. What we want to know is, 'Is it right or wrong?' but often the answer we get is: 'It all depends!' and sometimes you find the answer varies according to the person you have asked.

3 **Relativism.** Explain that this way of thinking about right and wrong is called 'relativism'. There are no hard and fast rules for anything. It all depends ... on the person, the time, the situation. There are no 'absolutes'. In other words, there is nothing that is *always* right or *always* wrong. One person's good is another person's bad and one person's right is another person's wrong. The best thing we can be, it seems, is tolerant.

4 Give the following illustration of why relativism doesn't work (or think of another example to make the same point):

• Comment that if you were to say to them that since the assembly began, there had been one person who had continually been picking his nose, they might respond that it's a free country and who says it's wrong anyway? We need to be tolerant.

However, if you said that since the start of the assembly, someone had been going along the back row sticking a knife into people, then they probably *wouldn't* say that it's a free country or ask who says it's wrong anyway. There is an end to our tolerance! Immediately, we have an absolute – killing is wrong! Relativism doesn't work.

5 Utilitarianism. Explain that other people say that we can agree, as a society, on what is right and what is wrong. We can come to a consensus. This is called 'utilitarianism'. Right and wrong are decided by what the majority of the people believe is right or wrong. The problem with this idea is that the majority of the people at a given time may think, for example, that a policy of ethnic cleansing or genocide is right. Or the crucifixion of an innocent man ...

Application

1 The confusion surrounding what is right and what is wrong has sometimes been referred to as 'the moral maze' or even a 'moral crisis'. People aren't sure any more if there are any rights or wrongs!

2 Christians believe that God, as the creator of the world, has the best plan for how it should work and how we should live. They believe that, in some ways, the Bible can be a guidebook, a manual for life. God's laws (or commandments) provide some absolutes that we can hold on to in a confusing and changing world.

3 Conclude by suggesting to pupils that they:

• spend some time thinking through exactly how they make up their minds about what is right and what is wrong.

• give some serious consideration as to whether the Bible could help them in finding out the right way to live.

11 TEN COMMANDMENTS FOR TODAY

aim

To challenge pupils to think about the moral code they live by.

Bible base

Exodus 20:3-17
– the ten commandments;

Luke 10:25-37
– love your neighbour as you love yourself.

You will need:

- An OHP
- 2 OHP acetates prepared as follows:
    OHP 1 – 'ten commandments for today' (see **Content** below)
    OHP 2 – God's ten commandments taken from Exodus 20:3-17 (see **Content** below)

Content

1 Ask the pupils what they would say if it was up to them to design the rules for life on earth – a kind of ten commandments for today. Would they make every day a Saturday? Would they put a McDonalds on every corner? Would they make all people equal?

2 Explain that some time ago, a poll was carried out by MORI and Radio 1, to find out more about the moral code that young people live by today. As a result, the following 'ten commandments for today' was drawn up **(display OHP 1)**. The percentage of young people who agreed with the 'commandment' is shown in brackets.

Do not kill. *(87%)*
Do not drink and drive. *(79%)*
Do not steal. *(73%)*
Treat others as yourself. *(71%)*
Do not use violence. *(70%)*
Do not be racist. *(68%)*
Care for the environment. *(64%)*
Do not take drugs. *(60%)*
Be loyal to your friends. *(55%)*
Do not commit adultery. *(53%)*

3 It's encouraging that we are still able today to arrive at a moral code, and that there does seem to be some agreement about what is right and wrong. Perhaps that's an indication that our God-given consciences are still at work. But still only three out of four believe that stealing is wrong and only about half of those asked said adultery was wrong.

4 Compare this survey with the original – God's ten commandments **(display OHP 2)**.

Worship no God but me.

Do not bow down to any idol or worship it.

Do not take the Lord's name in vain.

Remember the Sabbath and keep it holy.

Honour your father and mother.

Do not commit murder.

Do not commit adultery.

Do not steal.

Do not accuse anyone falsely.

Do not desire anything your neighbour has.

5 Although they are separated by around 3500 years, the two sets of commandments are actually very similar. Many of them focus on how we treat one another – a bit like the command, 'Love your neighbour as yourself' which Jesus taught his hearers about in the parable of the good Samaritan (Luke 10:25-37).

6 Some of God's commandments seem to have been lost, like the ones about swearing, Sundays and wanting what others have got. But the 'ten commandments for today' also include things that God would agree with, like caring for the environment and not taking drugs.

7 What's missing from these modern commandments is *God!* Rather than God, the young people in the survey mentioned respected celebrities (eg Richard Branson, Mother Teresa) as being the sort of people who give a moral lead.

Application

1 Christians would say that the danger of this is that if the foundation of our moral code is based on what or who happens to be in fashion at the time and not the unchanging words of God, then it is unstable. The message of the Bible is that when we are faced with moral decisions, but don't rely on God's commandments as a base for our lives or to guide us, the results are likely to be confusion, chaos and moral decline – just the situation some would say we have today!

2 It's encouraging that many people *do* have a moral code that they try to live by. The problem is, to do just that! Someone once said, 'God's commandments are not too difficult for us – they're impossible!' Breaking rules, even our own rules, seems to be what we're best at!

3 Christians believe that that is why Jesus came. He was the only one who ever kept the commandments. And because he was blameless, he could be the one who took the blame, so that we could have our failures of the past wiped clean, and then have his help to live his way in the future. Christians try to love and value other people – because they realise how much God has loved and valued them!

12 THE GRAB

aim

To challenge pupils to think about the moral code they live by.

Bible base

Luke 12:16-21 – the rich fool;

Mark 10:17-31 – the rich young ruler.

You will need:

- A tray with a selection of three or four chocolate bars and some 'undesirable' objects (eg a used match, an old comb, a biro that's run out, a snapped elastic band). As one of the 'undesirable' objects include a lump of dirty *Blu-tack* which is wrapped around and conceals a one pound coin.
- The name of the game, 'The Grab', displayed on an OHP acetate (or large piece of card)

Content

The Grab

1 Ask for three or four volunteers to come to the front. Explain to them that they will be shown a tray with a selection of objects on it. At a given signal you want them to grab whatever they want from the selection of 'goodies'.

2 Explain to them that the idea of the game is simply to take what they want, before someone else does. After all, isn't that the whole point of life?

3 Explain that you will count down ('Three, two, one ... ') and then, they are to grab! If someone else gets what they wanted, they must go for something else quickly. Increase the drama by stopping the countdown a couple of times to restrain any over-eager 'grabbers' who are trying to start too soon.

4 When 'The Grab' is over, and the volunteers have their choices, talk to them about whether they are happy about what they wanted, the reasons for their choices etc.

5 Explain that sometimes it's better not to go for the things in the nicest packaging. For example, once you've eaten the chocolate bars, you'll soon be hungry again! Then pick up the *Blu-tack* and reveal that concealed inside this very ordinary and not very attractive object, there is hidden treasure – a one pound coin. This one object could buy four or five of the things they grabbed.

Make the point that to have opted for the dirty *Blu-tack* or one of the other 'undesirable' things would probably have seemed odd to everyone else, because in our society the best packaging, the way things look on the outside and 'image' are very important to us.

6 Ask the volunteers to return to their seats. They can keep what they 'grabbed'.

Application

1 Tell the pupils that Jesus had a lot to say on the subject of priorities. Read to them from a contemporary version of the Bible the story of the rich fool (Luke 12:16-21).

2 Explain that Jesus himself had no home and very few possessions, but he didn't ever seem jealous of the rich people he met. In fact, he seemed to feel sorry for them because that was all they had – their riches; and he knew that they couldn't see beyond them. The danger was that the wealth they believed to be so important, would only bring them disappointment. (See also Mark 10:17-31 – the story of the rich young ruler.)

3 Comment that perhaps some of them have already noticed that the 'richest' people they know don't necessarily have lots of money or attractive possessions. Instead, they have decided to make the sort of person they are on the inside their priority, and that's infinitely more precious than wealth and outward appearances.

4 Conclude by challenging pupils to decide what their priorities for life are going to be.

13 CHOICES, CHOICES

aim

To help pupils realise that they have the freedom to choose between right and wrong; to challenge them to have the courage to 'go against the flow'.

Bible base

Matthew 7:13,14
– the narrow gate.

You will need:

- An OHP
- An OHP acetate – a drawing of a little fish which is swimming in the opposite direction to a huge shoal of fish (see illustration)
- Items for the 'choices' exercise (see **Content** below)
- A prize

Content

Choices

1 Ask some pupils in the audience to choose between two things you offer them (eg two different flavour chewy bars; two different colour biros; a *Mars* or a *Snickers* Bar).

2 Comment that we are all used to this sort of choice, for example when we go shopping. This kind of choosing can be very enjoyable.

3 Continue by saying that there are, however, many things in life where we *don't* have a choice (eg where we are born, the colour of our skin, the family we are part of etc). There are also things we have *some* influence over, but not much (which school we go to, which class we are in, which teacher we have). But that still leaves many areas of life where we are free to make our own choices.

4 Comment that it's worth remembering that even if we don't make a decision, we are still making a choice. We are choosing that we'll drift along through life, being pushed and pulled in all sorts of directions by whoever and whatever has the strongest influence on us at the time.

It's hard to be different

1 Say to the pupils that it's hard not to do what everyone else does. Announce that you are about to demonstrate this.

2 Ask the front row of pupils to stand up. Ask them to go to one side of the room, but ask one person to stay with you on the opposite side of the room. Ask those in the group to walk – as a group – across the front of the hall. Ask the person on their own to try to walk through them. It's difficult. Be prepared to step in to avoid injury!

3 Ask them all to sit down. Give the pupil who walked across the room on their own a prize.

4 Display the drawing of the fish on the OHP acetate.

5 Say that it is difficult to stand out from the crowd. It needs real strength. Sometimes we 'go with the flow' just to survive! But 'going against the flow' may have benefits! After all, it's possible that the crowd is wrong! Those fish may be going in the wrong direction, perhaps even to their destruction!

6 Comment that, to a large extent, all of us get our ideas of what everyone else does and thinks from the media – TV and magazines. However, that is actually a very limited picture of what people do and think – it only represents *this* part of the world at *this* moment in time. 'Everybody does it', or 'everybody says so' is usually not a very well-founded claim! But even if it were true that 'everybody does it', it's still not reasonable to think that you have to do it as well.

7 The fact that it's difficult not to do something, doesn't mean you don't have a choice.

For example, you are at a party where it seems as if everyone is drinking excessively and getting drunk. You have a choice:

- you can join in and get drunk;
- you can leave the party;
- you can stay at the party but not drink.

Comment that the first option is the easiest. You could do this without having to think at all. The other options require you to do some thinking, to make a decision, and then stick by that decision – no matter what other people might say. But don't deceive yourself by thinking that there is *no* choice.

Application

1 Ask the pupils to listen to these words of Jesus: 'The gate to hell is wide and the road that leads to it is easy, and there are many who travel it. But the gate to life is narrow and the way that leads to it is hard, and there are few people who find it' (Matthew 7:13,14, *Good News Bible*).

2 Comment that – when it comes to making choices about right and wrong – it isn't easy to go in the opposite direction to most other people, especially if you feel as if you are on your own in the choice you have made.

3 Conclude with a few moments of quiet. Ask the pupils to think about the choices that face them. Ask if there are any areas of their lives where they are 'going with the flow' when really, they want to go against it.

14 EMBARRASSING!

aim

To show pupils that being embarrassed may be a price worth paying for doing what's right.

Bible base

2 Kings 5:1-15 – the story of Naaman.

Preparation

• Find out in advance if there is a teacher who would be willing to tell the pupils about their most embarrassing experience (optional).

• Prepare and rehearse your telling of the story of Naaman (see 2 Kings 5:1-15). Aim to make it as entertaining as possible, emphasising any 'embarrassing' aspects.

Content

Introduction

Talk about how embarrassing it could be for you taking an assembly in front of all of them! You might make a mistake, or say the wrong thing, or forget what to say completely. So, you are relying on everyone to help you.

A survey

1 Announce that you are going to conduct a survey on the subject of embarrassment. Tell the pupils sitting on the front row of the assembly that you would like them to help you. (You need a group of about fifteen to twenty people.)

2 Say that you are going to give them a series of two alternatives. Each of the options will be represented by opposite sides side of the hall. They must each decide which of the two alternatives is the most embarrassing situation and move to the appropriate side of the hall. Insist that they must make their own decisions.

3 The choices are:

• being singled out by name in assembly *or* to go forward as a group to receive an award;

• falling flat on your face in some mud *or* being drenched by a passing car going through a puddle;

• making the alarm go off in Marks & Spencer's doorway *or* not having enough money to pay at the supermarket (you could use the name of the local supermarket) checkout;

• getting bottom marks in a test *or* getting top marks in a test;

• being seen by your friends with a member of the opposite sex *or* being seen by your friends out shopping with your parents;

• photos of you from four or five years ago being shown to relatives at a family party *or* everyone at the party being told how well you are doing at school.

4 When the survey is complete, thank those who took part and ask them to return to their seats.

How embarrassing!

1 Make the point that whilst some of them might have found it embarrassing to come to the front, at least they had other people with them! The most embarrassing times are when you feel as if everyone knows that you alone have done something stupid! For example:

• An American – Tony Randall – who had been asked to be a spokesman for the National Sleep Disorder Month, over-slept and missed a guest spot on the TV show *Wake up America*.

• Police were called to a flat in Bournemouth after a passer-by heard screams of 'Help!' They found twenty-one year old Toni Hoare in the shower, singing along to the Beatles' song of the same title at the top of her voice!

• Tell the audience about one of the most embarrassing moments you have experienced and/or ask a teacher to do this.

2 These are all situations where the embarrassment has been due to a simple mistake. But there is another kind of embarrassment – the sort of embarrassment you know you are going to feel because you have chosen to do or say something unusual because you believe it is right or necessary.

3 As an illustration, tell the story of Naaman dramatically, drawing out all the embarrassing aspects. Explain that Naaman was a very important man with lots of servants. Unfortunately, he had a serious skin disease – leprosy. He reluctantly agreed to God's way of curing him. Emphasise how embarrassing it must have been going to bathe not once, but seven times, one after the other, in a not-very-beautiful river, especially in front of all his servants.

Conclude your telling of the story by saying that he obviously thought the embarrassment of doing something so apparently stupid was worth it for the sake of being cured.

Application

1 People sometimes find it difficult to admit they are a Christian, or even to show that they are interested in the Christian faith. They are afraid they will be teased or ridiculed – and, as a result, embarrassed.

2 Continue by saying that many people throughout history have taken risks and been ridiculed for something they believed in (eg believing that the earth was round; that penicillin was an effective medicine; that the sun was the centre of the solar system). And sometimes the cost of doing what you believe in can be far worse than embarrassment – it can be persecution or even death. That is still happening to some people today, just for admitting that they are Christians.

3 Conclude by saying that sometimes it's difficult to do what's right, especially when most people act as if they think you are wrong. It takes courage to stand up for what you believe in, but the temporary embarrassment may be a price worth paying for doing what is right.

15 WHO IS THE GREATEST?

aim

To show pupils that in God's eyes, the greatest of all is the servant of all.

Bible base

Mark 9:35
– the last will be first;
John 13:1-17 – Jesus washes the disciples' feet.

You will need:

- Some sheets of A4 paper for making paper aeroplanes
- A bowl of water and a towel for the feet washing exercise

Content

Introduction

1 Ask the pupils: 'Who is the greatest?' Say that for some people the answer might be ... (say the name of a popular, successful football team); or for someone else it might be ... (say the name of a singer or group who has recently had a number one hit). Give one or two examples of your own favourite celebrities – possibly provoking some groans from the audience!

2 Comment that everyone will have a different answer, according to their interests and allegiances.

3 Continue by asking, 'But who is the greatest here?' Say that today, you are going to find out.

The great aeroplane contest

1 Ask for three or four volunteers to take part in a 'Who is the greatest?' contest.

2 Explain that you want the volunteers to make a paper aeroplane from the A4 paper provided. They will then launch their aeroplanes from a raised point in the room (eg standing on a chair, or on the stage). The winner ('the greatest') will be the person whose paper plane travels the furthest.

3 Act as commentator whilst the contestants make their planes, building up the excitement and drama of the contest. When they are ready, ask each competitor to launch their planes in turn. Ask the audience to allow each plane to land and then the pupil nearest should pick up the aeroplane and hold it aloft

as a 'marker' showing the next contestant the distance he/she must try to beat.

4 When the contest is over, announce the winner and reward them with a 'tremendous' prize (hand them a sheet of A4 paper) – an aeroplane! Give everyone a round of applause. Keep your volunteers at the front. Ask the winner how it feels to be the greatest (great designer, great scientist, great inventor and great test pilot) – officially!

Application

1 Comment that it's a good feeling to be 'the greatest', getting all the glory and lots of attention. Then say that the Bible has something to say on the subject. Read these words from the Gospel of Mark: 'Whoever wants to be first must place himself last of all and be the servant of all' (Mark 9:35, *Good News Bible*). Say that this seems a strange way to describe greatness.

2 Jesus' way of looking at things is not the same as ours. On one occasion he demonstrated this to his disciples by getting down on his hands and knees and washing their feet! An amazing thing to do – as you can imagine – considering they were living in a hot country and had been wearing sandals.

Jesus said that he expected his disciples to do the same sort of things for one another, and that the most important people actually live as though they are the least important!

3 Bring out the bowl of water and the towel and ask the winner of the paper aeroplane contest how he/she feels – considering that they are 'the greatest person' here – about washing the feet of the losers.

If the winner agrees, let him/her do this! If they are obviously uncomfortable about doing it, take the heat out of the situation by saying that we don't have to wash one another's feet literally! Whatever your 'winner' decides to do, point out that there are lots of other ways we can act as servants to one another (give some examples).

4 Comment that when people are asked to list those who they consider to be great, today or in the past, those included are nearly always people who have served others in some way.

5 Challenge 'the winner', and everyone else, to think of how they could serve others today.

16 CLAY IN THE POTTER'S HANDS

aim

To explore the relevance to pupils of God's message given through the Old Testament prophet, Jeremiah.

Bible base

Jeremiah 13:1-11 – muddy shorts;
Jeremiah 18:1-4 – clay in the potter's hands;
Jeremiah 24:1,2 – bowls of fruit.

You will need:

- Playdough or similar material
- 3 trays
- a bowl of rotten fruit
- a bowl of fresh fruit
- 2 pairs of boxer shorts (one muddy pair, one clean pair)
- an attractive vase made of pottery
- 3 prizes

Preparation

- Find out in advance if there is an art teacher in the school who would be willing to 'judge' the clay modelling.

Content

Introductory activity

1 Ask for three volunteers to come to the front. Give them each a lump of playdough and tell them you would like them to make the following: one has to make a sugar bowl (with a lid); one a milk jug; and one a vase.

2 Get them to sit down to do this on one side of the front area, while you speak to everyone else.

Talk about Jeremiah

1 Say to the pupils that you are going to tell them about a man called Jeremiah, who we can read about in the Bible. Explain

that he was a prophet (someone who tells people God's messages and speaks God's words) from the time he was twenty years old until he was fifty.

2 He wasn't very popular. Today we still use his name in a derogatory way. An 'Old Jeremiah' is someone who is always moaning. He is the sort of person you might think of seeing with a sandwich board in front of him, saying, 'Repent! The end is nigh!' It's true that Jeremiah did have some hard messages from God: 'Turn away from your evil ways'; 'Stop your idolatry'; 'Put God first'; 'Do what he wants'; 'What God says will come about ... there will be judgment!'

3 As a result, and not surprisingly, Jeremiah wasn't liked. He was mocked, laughed at and plotted against. Even so, he must have been very courageous to say such hard things to people.

4 Although his preaching was about very serious matters, Jeremiah often used humour to help people understand what God wanted to say to them about how they should live. Here are some of the illustrations he used.

A BOWL OF ROTTEN FRUIT

1 At this point, offer the bowl of rotten fruit to pupils near the front and watch for their reactions. They will probably refuse!

2 Explain that God was saying to the people of Israel (and to people today) that they were like the rotten fruit. They had gone off! They weren't what they were meant to be. (Give some examples relevant to the pupils, to illustrate ways in which people's lives are 'rotten' and not what God intended them to be.)

A BOWL OF FRESH FRUIT

1 Offer the good fruit to pupils and let two or three take a piece.

2 Explain that God was giving a picture through this illustration of how the Israelites' (or our) lives could be if they (we) would follow him and live his way. (Give some examples.)

SOME UNDERPANTS

1 Ask if there is a boy who would be willing to come to the front to model some clothes for you. When you have a volunteer warn him that you are going to ask him a very personal question. Ask: *Do you prefer Y fronts or boxers?* Whatever the

answer, ask him to choose a pair of boxers from the two pairs you show him. One pair is clean; the other pair is muddy. He will probably choose the clean pair! He must then try them on (over his trousers, of course!).

2 Explain that God was saying through this illustration that he wants to be as close to people as a pair of 'undies'! Unfortunately, the Israelites (us too?) were like a pair of 'undies' that had been buried in the ground for a while. So they weren't very pleasant and weren't much use.

3 Jeremiah said that God was longing for people to turn to him, so that they would enjoy a much better life. Sadly, they were too rebellious and wouldn't listen to Jeremiah or God.

THE MODELLING CLAY

1 Turn back to your original volunteers, who have by now, hopefully, finished making their different models. Ask them to step forward and show their work.

2 Before you examine what they have made, say that you have with you a vase that you made earlier out of the same material. (Make sure the audience understands from the way you speak that this isn't really true!) Bring out an attractive pottery vase as the standard against which their work will be judged. If possible, ask an art teacher to help you award points.

3 Whatever the results, give everyone a prize.

4 Then ask the contestants some questions about their work. For example:

- Are you happy with what you have made?
- Would you mind putting your name on it?
- Did the playdough behave as you wanted?
- Would you like to start again, given the chance?

If anyone says, 'Yes' to this last question, screw their clay up and give it back to them.

5 Explain that for this last illustration God took Jeremiah to a pottery. There he saw that if there was an impurity, a flaw, or something going wrong in the potter's work, it would be broken down and the potter would start again. Then, when the pot was finished, the potter was happy to put his mark of ownership on it. The potter would keep on working on his pot until he had made something that was not only beautiful, but useful as well.

6 God was saying through Jeremiah that he is like the potter, and his people, the Israelites, were like the clay.

Application
1 Explain that a Christian is a bit like someone who is prepared to be like clay in God's hands.
2 Challenge pupils to think about what their lives are like (a bowl of rotten fruit? a bowl of fresh fruit? not-very-clean boxer shorts?). Who or what is in control of the way they live. Ask them to consider letting God (the potter) have a part in shaping their lives (the clay).

17 THE MOST POWERFUL THING IN THE WORLD

aim

To challenge pupils to consider the power of the words they speak – to hurt or to help others.

Bible base

Proverbs 10:18; 11:13; 16:28; 18:8; 26:20 – don't gossip;

James 3:1-12 – the power of the tongue.

You will need:

- A tube of toothpaste
- A plate
- A banana
- Sellotape
- An OHP and 6 OHP acetates (or cards) to show Persian proverb and words from the book of Proverbs (see **Preparation** and **Content** below)
- A CD or tape of music and appropriate equipment to play it on

Preparation

- Prepare OHP acetates (or cards) in advance, showing words as follows (quotations from Proverbs are taken from the *Good News Bible*):

OHP 1 – 'An arrow that has left the bow never returns.' – a Persian proverb.

OHP 2 – 'A man who hides his hatred is a liar. Anyone who spreads gossip is a fool.' – Proverbs 10:18.

OHP 3 – 'No one who gossips can be trusted with a secret, but you can put confidence in someone who is trustworthy.' – Proverbs 11:13.

OHP 4 – 'Gossip is spread by wicked people; they stir up trouble and break up friendships.' – Proverbs 16:28.

OHP 5 – 'Gossip is so tasty – how we love to swallow it'. – Proverbs 18:8.

OHP 6 – 'Without wood, a fire goes out; without gossip, quarrelling stops.' – Proverbs 26:20.

- Work out in advance a thirty second excerpt of music which will act as a timer in the introductory activity. Set up your equipment for playing the music before the assembly begins and check that it works as you intend.

Content

That's impossible!

1 Ask for two volunteers. Ask one volunteer to squirt some toothpaste onto the plate. Ask the other volunteer to unpeel the banana.

2 Then tell them they have thirty seconds to put the toothpaste back in the tube and to seal up the banana with the sellotape. Play an excerpt from a music CD or tape to time them.

3 At the end of the thirty seconds, show the audience how they've got on. After a round of applause, ask them to return to their seats.

4 Comment that really, that was an impossible task. Then **display OHP 1** showing the Persian proverb: 'An arrow that has left the bow never returns.'

5 Explain that just like the squeezed-out toothpaste, a peeled banana and an arrow that has left the bow, so it is with words, once we've said them, we can't take them back.

Words can hurt

Tell the following funny story to make the serious point about how words can hurt, and the need to think about the effect of our words on others:

> There was once a lady on a train with her baby. A man came into the same compartment. He looked at the baby and said, 'That is the ugliest baby I have ever seen!' And he started to laugh uncontrollably. He got off the train at the next station. Another man got on and came and sat in the same compartment. There, he found the lady who was obviously very upset. He tried to get her to say what the matter was, but she couldn't speak because she was crying so much. So, at the next station, he leapt out of the carriage, ran to a shop, and managed to get back just as the train was pulling out. 'There, there,' he said, 'please don't cry. Here, I've bought you a drink and some tissues. And look, I've even bought a banana for your monkey!'*

Those were not the right words!

* Source of story unknown.

Small but powerful

1 The Bible says that the tongue – that small part of us which plays such a powerful role in producing our words – is a bit like the rudder of a big ship: relatively small but very influential. Or, it is like a little spark in a forest that can cause a huge fire (see James 3:4-6)!

2 You can use your tongue to discourage others. Demonstrate this by suddenly saying something insulting to someone on the front row. (Try to pick someone who looks as if they won't be hurt by your 'insult' and make sure that the audience under-stands you are joking!)

3 You can also use your tongue to encourage (eg: 'You know, I think you were really good when you did that!'). It costs nothing to use our words to build someone else up – instead of ourselves!

Don't gossip!

If you've ever had any gossip spread about you, you'll know how hurtful it can be. The Bible has some particularly useful things to say about gossip in a book of wise sayings called The Book of Proverbs. See if you can see the wisdom in these words:

• **Display OHP 2:** 'Anyone who spreads gossip is a fool.' Ask: *Is this true?*

• **Display OHP 3:** 'No one who gossips can be trusted.' Ask: *Is this true?* Comment that if it is, then so is the first proverb. People who can't be trusted end up not having many friends. God warns us against gossip because he wants us to have friends!

• **Display OHP 4:** 'Gossip is spread by wicked people; they stir up trouble and break up friendships.' Ask: *Can you think of an occasion when that has happened?*

• **Display OHP 5:** 'Gossip is so tasty – how we love to swallow it!' Ask: *Is this true?* Begin to tell a bit of 'juicy' imaginary gossip. Then stop abruptly and draw pupils' attention to how carefully people are listening all of a sudden!

• **Display OHP 6:** 'Without wood, a fire goes out; without gossip, quarrelling stops.' Ask: *Why not put that to the test?*

Three important questions

1 A group of people called the Quakers are renowned for not saying much at all, especially in their church services. But they have a rule of thumb about the way they try to use words when speaking about someone else. They ask themselves these questions before they speak:

- Is it true?
- Is it kind?
- Is it necessary?

2 Challenge pupils to see if they can follow this 'rule' today: to remember – before they speak – to ask themselves those three questions.

Application

1 Say that you have *spoken* enough!

2 Conclude with a few moments of quiet. Explain that you want pupils to use this time to think about the way they have used words in the past, and how they are going to speak, today.

18 SOAP

aim

To help pupils understand that just as we need to be made clean on the outside, so God wants us to be made 'clean' on the inside.

Bible base

Mark 7:20-23
– 'dirty' on the inside.

You will need:

- 5 different brands of soap
- A 'smellograph' score chart on OHP acetate or card (see illustration)
- A copy of 'Reasons why I never wash' on OHP acetate or card (see **Content** below)
- 2 or 3 blindfolds
- A small prize (eg a bar of soap or sponge)

SMELLOGRAPH			
Names of Contestants			
DOVE			
PALMOLIVE			
IMPERIAL LEATHER			
FAIRY			
ARIEL			

Preparation

- Prepare OHP acetates (or cards) as suggested.

Content

Introduction

1 Begin by saying that if you were to mention the word 'soap', many people would immediately think of *Home and Away* or *Coronation Street*, but actually, there is another meaning of the word! Soap is something we use to wash with!

At Christmas or for birthdays, one of the most popular gifts is soap. Comment that you are not sure what we are trying to say to our friends and relatives about their personal hygiene, but obviously, making ourselves and our loved ones clean and smelling nice, is a favourite national pastime!

2 Explain that the very first soap was made in the Nile valley around 600BC and carried by Phoenician seamen all around the Mediterranean coastline. Soap is actually a substance made by the action of alkali on fat. Most of us don't care about that, we just want the right colour and fragrance.

The 'smellograph'

1 Display the 'smellograph' score chart.

2 Explain that you are going to have a competition. Ask for two or three volunteers. Blindfold them and explain that they are going to have to smell five different brands of soaps (eg *Dove, Palmolive, Imperial Leather, Fairy* washing-up liquid, *Ariel* washing powder). To make it easier, you could tell them in advance the five brands they have to choose from. The winner will be the contestant who can recognise the most brands of soap correctly.

3 In turn, ask the contestants to smell the different soap brands one at a time. Record their verdicts on the 'smellograph'.

4 When the contest is complete, take off the blindfolds, reveal the results and award the winning contestant a prize of a bar of soap, or a sponge!

Reasons why I never wash

Ask the pupils whether they think our national obsession with cleanliness is really necessary. Tell them that one young person didn't think so. He gave these reasons for why he never washed **(display the 'Reasons why I never wash' list** on OHP acetate or card) :

- I was made to wash when I was little, but I got bored with it, so I stopped.
- None of my friends get washed. I'd look stupid if I started!
- I haven't got the time.
- I still get washed on special occasions, like Christmas and Easter!
- The bathroom's always too cold!
- Maybe when I'm older, I'll start getting washed. I've got plenty of time.
- There are so many different brands of soap. How do you know which one to choose?
- People who wash are hypocrites – they reckon they're cleaner than other people.
- People who make soap are only after your money!*

Application

1 Point out how silly these reasons for not washing are. We all need to be clean. Life wouldn't be anywhere near as pleasant if we all stopped washing!

2 The Bible makes it clear that it's not just on the outside that we need to be made clean. It talks about our wrong attitudes, actions and thoughts (called 'sin'), which make us unclean and keep us separated from a holy, pure God. The Bible also talks about Jesus, who was born in a dirty stable, in a dirty world, and who wants to clean up people's lives on the inside.

3 Comment that it is interesting that people often give very similar reasons for saying 'no' to God, as the young person gave for saying 'no' to soap. Ask the pupils to look again at 'The reasons why' list, and try to replace the references to soap and bathrooms with God, the Church and being cleaned up on the inside.

4 Conclude with a few moments of quiet for pupils to read through and think about 'The reasons why' list in the way you have suggested.

*This list is adapted from material published by Christian Publicity Organisation, Worthing. Leaflet CPO929 *10 reasons why I never wash* available from CPO. (Address at back of book.)

19 THE CHANCE TO START AGAIN

aim

To help pupils understand that God loves us – even when we feel we are 'failures', and he wants to help us make a fresh start.

Bible base

Mark 14:50
– the disciples desert Jesus;
John 18:15-18, 25-27
– Peter lets Jesus down;
John 21:15-19
– Jesus reinstates Peter.

Preparation

• This assembly idea is intended as a talk outline. Memorise the content, using words and expressions that you are comfortable with.
• Rehearse your presentation.

Content

We all make mistakes.

1 Begin by saying that there's one thing you can be sure of: we all make mistakes. We all have times when we feel as if the eyes of the whole world are watching us and as if everyone is saying, 'You're a failure. How could you be so stupid?!'

2 Tell your audience the following stories (or other examples) about some people who must have felt just like that:

• A lady was once appalled to find three teeth in a *Galaxy* Double Nut and Raisin bar. She complained to Mars (the firm that makes them) and her story got into *The Daily Star*. But when she went to her dentist, he told her that three of her back teeth were missing! She said, 'I feel such a fool!'

• A man who was originally from Barrow, in Cumbria, but who had then lived in Australia for thirty years, decided that the time was right to return to Britain in search of his long lost brother. So, he came home, only to discover that his brother had emigrated – to Australia!

• Army disposal experts were called in when a suspicious box was noticed outside Bristol Zoo. After the box was blown up, they discovered that it had contained a rat left by its owner, who had been hoping the zoo would give his pet a new home! The owner must have felt terrible.

3 Continue by saying that we all do things that make us feel we are failures. Sometimes they are silly things, mistakes we could have avoided. For example, in exams we sometimes go wrong because we don't read the question properly. Tell pupils one or two of the following exam 'mistakes' anecdotes:

• In answer to the question in her RE exam, 'Who was Noah's wife?' a girl wrote: 'Joan of Ark'!

• A boy was asked in a science exam, 'What is the boiling point of water?' His answer was: 'The point of boiling water is to make a cup of tea.'

• In another science exam, one task set was, 'Name an element.' Someone wrote: 'I name this element Arthur.'

No way back?

1 Say that the stories above are funny anecdotes to illustrate how we can all make silly mistakes. When we do, we probably wish we could have the time over again, then the next time we could avoid making the same mistake again. Sometimes though, the failure isn't just a 'silly mistake'. Things go wrong because we haven't done what we should have done (eg learnt our work in the first place, revised for an exam etc) and we've no one to blame but ourselves! Our failure is our own fault! We have made wrong decisions, had the wrong priorities and that's why we've failed.

When something like this happens, we can feel as if there is no way back: 'I am a failure – for the rest of my life!'

2 Tell your audience about a man called Peter. (Don't say immediately that you are talking about the disciple, Peter.) He felt a failure. He had let his best friend down – someone who would never let him down. His friend was arrested and ended up being executed for a crime he hadn't committed. Peter felt miserable and a total failure. After all, he'd run away and pretended he didn't even know his best friend! He had just tried to save his own skin.

Then, in what seemed like a dream – but wasn't – he met his friend again; and his friend said, 'It's OK, I forgive you, you can start again; come on, this is what I want you to do ... ' That young man, Peter, went on to become one of the world's great leaders, eventually giving his own life for the cause his best friend died for. Conclude Peter's story by saying that many of them will have guessed that Peter's best friend was ... Jesus.

Application

1 Tell your audience you want them to remember this: 'failures' can start again. Say that it is an important thing to remember in school, but also in every other area of life.

2 In a maths exam when you know you've got the answer wrong, you can re-think the problem and cross or rub out your mistakes. But you can still tell there has been a mistake; you can still see where you went wrong. Alternatively, you can start a brand new, clean page. Then it's as though nothing ever happened.

3 In an amazing way, God does exactly that for people who come to him and say, 'I'm a failure. I got it wrong and I want to start again.' Peter couldn't literally 'rub out' what he had done in the past and in some ways it would stay with him for ever, but he knew he was forgiven. That meant he was free to start again and to begin living the way God wanted.

4 Conclude by saying that it's great to know that the things we have done and said wrong can be forgiven, and that we – like Peter – can start again. And it's all possible because Peter's best friend paid the price of our failure.

20 GENESIS

Note: This assembly assumes that pupils are familiar with the content of Genesis 1. In some schools this may be a realistic assumption; in other schools it might not be. Check with the school in advance, if you are not sure.

aim

To challenge pupils' assumptions about how successful the human race has been in achieving fulfilment without God.

Preparation

• This assembly idea is simply a reading. Learn it by heart and practise saying it from memory. If you find this difficult to do, still memorise the content as far as possible, so that you are free to look up from the reading as you present the material. Rehearse thoroughly.

Content

After the beginning

1 The reading:

> After the beginning, man began. And man said, 'Let there be a wheel.' And there was a wheel. And man saw that it was good and invented all sorts of vehicles, from wagons pulled by oxen to trains driven by the power of the piston; from carts pulled by ponies to planes pushed by jet engines. And the evening and the morning were the first era.
>
> And man said, 'Let the laboratories bring forth the cleansers, the labour-saving devices, maintenance-free equipment. Let them multiply in infinite variety.' And it was so. And man made self-cleaning ovens, frost-free refrigerators, remote-control lawn mowers, automatic washers and driers, electronic, transistorised, trouble-free equipment of every conceivable type.
>
> And man saw that it was good. And the evening and the morning were the second era. And man said, 'Let there be a new dimension to our vision, so that we can see what takes

place on the other side of the earth as well as in every corner of our countryside and cities. Let this television divide the night from the day for its viewers so that the night people may rule. Let it be a sign of the seasons and give information to all the earth.' And it was so. And man made great towers to send the vision on electromagnetic waves; and he made a lesser sound called radio to rule the day. And he set them in the pattern of life to divide the day into segments, the years into series, and the summers into repeats. And man saw that it was good, and the evening and the morning were the third era.

And man said, 'Let there be power from the building blocks of the universe. And man made the power by dividing the atom and called that power an atomic bomb. And man said, 'Let the power of the atom be channelled into one purpose – the guarantee of peace upon the earth.' And man saw that it was good. And man said, 'Let the power bring forth new methods of manufacturing goods for all men.' And the atom yielded its power to produce submarines, aircraft carriers and missiles, each yielding after its own kind. And man thought it was good. And the evening and the morning were the fourth era.

And man said, 'Let the men of science bring forth a craft that will break the power of gravity and fly above the earth in the open firmament of heaven.' And man created great space capsules, orbiting platforms, communications satellites, flying spy machines in order to explore the universe and keep track of its earth neighbours. Every invention brought forth abundantly after its kind and inspired new creations. And man saw that it was good and blessed it with new budgets saying, 'Be fruitful and multiply in the earth.' And the evening and the morning were the fifth era.

And man said, 'Let us make a machine in our own image, after our likeness, and let it do all our calculating for us, keep an accurate record of all our economic affairs, keep up-to-date on all scientific progress, store in its memory all facts about the earth and every individual moving thing on it.' So, man created computers in his own image. And man blessed them and said, 'Do all the work required of man, multiply formulas and equations to the end of the universe, take charge of the power of the atom, and compute the path of the speeding spacecraft.' And man saw everything that he had made, and behold, he thought it was very good. And the evening and the morning were the sixth day.

Thus all the modern world was completed with its hosts of ingenious devices. In the seventh era, man said, 'Now I will rest and enjoy the fruits of all my labours. But the screaming jets would not let him sleep, the gadgets and expanded vision gave him stomach ulcers, his unlimited powers kept him nervously suspicious of his neighbours, and what he had created in his own image gave him answers to questions he did not like. Having made all things for his comfort and enjoyment, man found himself still anxious and in trouble. Great and marvellous were his achievements, but they brought no peace to him or to the world. For in the beginning was God, who made man and made his heart to be restless until it finds its rest, not in man's inventions, but in the creator and ruler who created peace and bestows it upon those who believe in the one he sent.*

2 Sit down without further comment.

* T Eugene Coffin. Previously appeared in *Link up*, a Scripture Union in Schools publication.

SECTION 3

WHO IS JESUS?

21 IDENTIKIT

aim

To challenge pupils to consider for themselves these questions: Who is Jesus? What is he like?

You will need:

- An OHP
- 6 pictures of famous people (cut out from newspapers or magazines and photocopied onto 6 separate OHP acetates; try to find unusual angles)

Content

Guess who?

1 Ask for six volunteers to make two teams of three. Tell them that you want them to identify the famous people they are about to see on the OHP screen. Show each team two pictures, one after another, giving the team a few seconds to discuss before giving their answer.

2 Cut up two of the acetates which show famous faces, making sure the audience aren't able to see the pictures (but don't get the two different faces muddled up!). Then each team, in turn, tries to piece together one of the faces, working on this together around the OHP. This is harder than it seems, because it's easy to get the image the wrong way round! Allow a set time within which the teams must complete their tasks.

3 The winning team is the one which got most questions right, or pieced together the face in the shortest time. Applaud their efforts. Ask the teams to return to their seats.

Identikit

1 Make the point that these famous people can be recognised easily by their physical appearance, as well as by their actions. However, before photography was invented, famous people were recognised *only* by what they did or who they were.

2 How can we know what Jesus would look like? Say that Jesus has been portrayed as a freedom fighter, a clown, a deranged madman, as a weak, sickly character and as a messiah. Who was – or is – he? Obviously, we don't have a photograph of him because he lived 2000 years ago. But the impact of his life, death and resurrection on history is so huge that the beginning of the new millenium we are about to celebrate (are celebrating/have recently celebrated) is based around his birthday!

Application

1 When people try to imagine what Jesus is like, they sometimes picture someone like this: a tall man with long hair and a beard, who walks around wearing a dressing gown! We can't really know exactly what Jesus did – or does – look like.

2 Tell the pupils that if they want a true 'identikit' picture of Jesus, they need to read the records we have about him, written by four people who knew him well – Matthew, Mark, Luke and John. These accounts are found in the Bible. In that way they can get to know the man behind the face! Say that it's a bit like putting pieces of a jigsaw together. Unless they are prepared to do that, they could be involved in a case of mistaken identity!

22 ICHTHUS

aim

To explore with pupils the meaning of the Christian symbol of the fish; and to encourage them to think about the significance of Jesus – the man the symbol reminds us of.

You will need:

- An OHP
- OHP acetates prepared as follows:

  OHP 1 – to show a selection of symbols (see illustration)

  OHP 2 – to show a selection of well known abbreviations (eg RAC, RSPCA, POW, the EC, GCSE, HNC etc)

  OHP 3 – to show the 'ichthus' fish symbol, including the Greek letters (see illustration)

  OHP 4 – an overlay showing the Greek letters, words and their meanings, to place on top of the 'ichthus' drawing (see **Preparation** below)

Preparation

- Prepare the OHP acetates as described above. The Greek letters, words and meanings for the fish symbol are as follows:

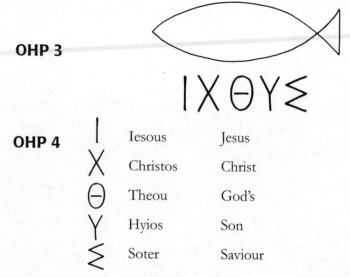

OHP 3

ΙΧΘΥΣ

OHP 4

Ι	Iesous	Jesus
Χ	Christos	Christ
Θ	Theou	God's
Υ	Hyios	Son
Σ	Soter	Saviour

OHP 1

Content

Symbols

1 **Display OHP 1**, revealing only the Woolmark symbol.

2 Say that today we are familiar with many different symbols and logos. They are used to remind people that a certain organisation, company or product exists. They are a kind of short-hand to take the place of the full name and are usually intended to communicate something about what the organisation or product does and about its 'image'.

3 Now uncover the whole of OHP 1 and ask the pupils to see how many of the logos they can identify.

4 Explain that sometimes the initials of an organisation, qualification etc are used either instead of or as part of a logo (eg

RAC stands for the Royal Automobile Club; GCSE stands for General Certificate of Secondary Education). Explain that abbreviations help us because, for example, 'GCSEs' is a lot easier to say than 'General Certificates of Secondary Education'.
5 Display OHP 2. Ask pupils how many of the abbreviations they can identify.

Ichthus
1 Display OHP 3 – the fish symbol. Ask if anyone knows what it stands for. Say that they might have seen one in the back window of a car.
2 Explain that in the early church, there were many years of persecution. In those days, to be a Christian, meant possible arrest and execution. During those times, Christians kept in touch with one another secretly. One of the methods they had for doing this was to leave the secret sign of the fish as a kind of 'password'.

This symbol was probably chosen because of Jesus' links with fishermen. The Greek word for 'fish' was 'ichthus'. Each letter making up that word was taken as the first letter of words which remind believers – and Christians ever since – of who Jesus is. **(Place OHP 4 – the overlay – on top of OHP 3.)** Say that, 'Jesus Christ, God's Son, our Saviour' was the meaning early Christians would think of when they saw the word 'ichthus'.
3 Explain that some Christians today put the fish symbol in the back window of their cars. It's a way of saying, 'I am a Christian' or 'I believe in what this symbol stands for', in much the same way as people put 'Save the Whale' or 'Give Blood' stickers in their car windows. It's a way of saying, 'I'm not ashamed of what I believe in.'

Displaying the fish symbol is also a way of doing what the early Christians did in much more difficult times – making contact with others who believe the same. When Christians see the fish it reminds them of what they have in common – a belief in Jesus Christ who is God's Son and our Saviour.
4 Encourage pupils to look out for the fish symbol. Challenge them – next time they see it – to try to remember the Greek word 'ichthus', what it means and what it tells them about Jesus.

23 HEROES

aim

To help pupils see that Jesus has all the best qualities of a hero – and more!

You will need:

- An OHP
- Pictures or photos of people who are regarded in some way as heroes (which could be taken from newspapers or magazines) photocopied onto OHP acetates of people who are regarded in some way as heroes (see **Content** below for suggestions)

Preparation

- Prepare OHP acetates as described above.
- The content of the **Application** section involves you in talking to pupils about your own faith in a personal way. Think especially carefully about how you will do this in a way which is appropriate to you and to your audience.

Content

1 Ask how many of them have seen Superman on TV. Comment that he has been a superhero now for about forty years – and he still looks so young! Mention some of the amazing things he can do – like change his clothes in mid-air!

2 Say that most people have a hero at some time. Briefly refer to your own childhood or current heroes.

3 Ask your audience: *What makes a hero?* Ask what it is that makes some people achieve that sort of status?

4 Continue by giving some examples of different kinds of 'hero'. As you talk, display the relevant pictures on the OHP. Use the suggestions below or other examples of the same type of 'heroes'. Make sure it is someone who the pupils will be familiar with. Say that their hero might be:

- someone you would like to be like (eg Princess Di or Alan Shearer);
- someone who expresses the sort of values you have (eg Michael Jackson or Richard Branson);

• someone who has qualities which you admire (eg Gary Lineker or the Queen);

• someone who has done something of great importance (eg Nelson Mandela);

• someone who has enormous influence over people (eg a currently popular super pop star or super model; or even someone like Adolf Hitler, because he was a hero to some people!);

• someone people treat with special reverence* (eg Mother Teresa).

5 Comment that there are some problems with having heroes. For example:

• You will probably never get to meet them. They are so far away, so distant. They might as well be on another planet, or in another world for the rich and famous. You are just one of their adoring fans at the concert, or the match, or in your lounge watching TV!

• Your heroes will never know you. Even if you did actually see your hero in the street and go rushing up to her or him, they wouldn't know you from Adam. That's one of the reasons that people in the public eye often keep a low profile, keeping away from the very people who love them, for fear of the maniac!

• And then what would it be like if you did actually get to meet your hero? Explain that you have a sneaking suspicion that it would probably be a bit of a disappointment, an anti-climax compared with the image you've created in your mind; compared with this person you've put on a pedestal. They won't, they can't live up to your expectations. Then they will fall from the dizzy heights where you have put them. You don't really know your hero; you only know the image presented by the media, not the real person, warts and all.

• This, of course, leads to the unpalatable but highly likely discovery that your hero doesn't really care about you. Of course, she or he is really nice and does love all the adoring fans, but not in an individual or practical way. After all, heroes couldn't care about everyone like that, could they?

6 Comment that all heroes are human and prone to the same

---

* The categories of heroes listed here are suggested in *Heroes*, Ruth Harrison, Lion.

inadequacies as everyone else. Explain that you are not saying people shouldn't have heroes; it's just important to remember that they, like everyone else, are not perfect and so are always likely to let you down.

Application

Note: See comment in **Preparation** above.

1 Say that you have a hero who is different from any other. Explain that, as a Christian, you believe that Jesus – who's been a hero for 2000 years – fits all the criteria of the hero perfectly:

- he is someone you would like to be like;
- he expresses the values you want to live by;
- he has qualities you admire;
- he has done something of the greatest importance;
- he has a good influence over people;
- he is treated with reverence.

2 Comment that maybe there are other people you could say that of, but the quality of Jesus' life goes beyond what mere human beings – even really good human beings – can do.

3 Christians believe that he is a hero who knows each of us better than we can know him, or even ourselves. In fact, he is the one who approaches us, wanting our friendship. Say that as you've got to know him, you have found that he cares about you to the extent that he's stuck by you through the bad times, instead of you – the hero worshipper – sticking by him, unlike most hero/fan relationships.

4 Amazingly, although he's got millions of fans, you are able to meet him every day, because he's always so approachable. For the Christian, this is a spiritual experience, but you know that you can look forward to heaven, when you believe you will meet him face to face. And when you do, rather than being an anti-climax or a let-down, it will be mind blowing!

5 Conclude by saying that it's a privilege to have a world famous hero who is also your best friend!

24 TRAPPED!

Note: This assembly is most suitable for use with upper school pupils.

aim

To explore with pupils the nature of authority, especially that of Jesus; to challenge them to think about who and what is in control of their lives

Bible base
Romans 7:18,19
– I want to do what's right, but ...

You will need:

- A chair
- A ball of wool
- A pair of scissors
- An OHP
- OHP acetates prepared as follows:
  OHP 1 – pictures of people in authority (see illustration)
  OHP 2 – picture of teenager with ball and chain (see illustration)
  OHP 3 – picture of man ignoring warning sign (see illustration)
  OHP 4 – words of the song *It's a sin* by The Pet Shop Boys (optional)
  OHP 5 – the words from Romans 7:18,19 (use the *Good News Bible* version)
  OHP 6 – picture showing the empty tomb of Jesus (see illustration)
- CD or tape of the song *It's a sin* by The Pet Shop Boys and appropriate equipment to play it on (optional)

Preparation

- Prepare OHP acetates as described above.

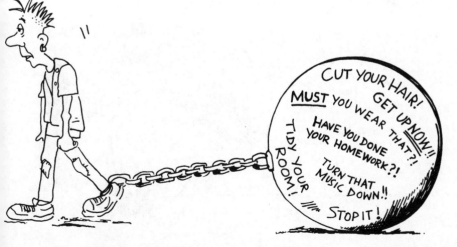

OHP 3

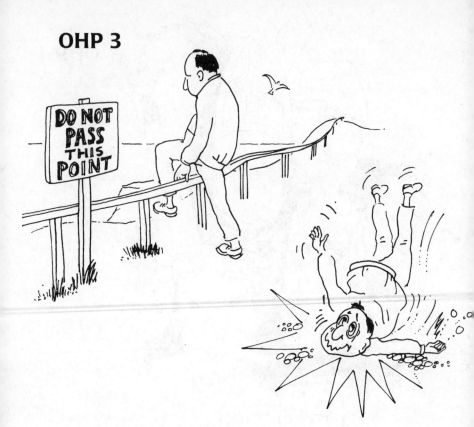

OHP 6

Content

Introduction

Begin with a short game of 'Simon says'. Ask pupils to do some odd things (but nothing which is too embarrassing!).

Who's in charge?

1 Say that sometimes it feels strange when someone tells us to do something. Point out that, even so, some people do have the authority to do that. Ask the pupils to call out some examples (eg teachers, parents, the police, the government). **Display OHP 1.**

2 Sometimes people have authority over us because they are working for our good, or for the greatest good of the greatest number. Sometimes people with authority have been appointed or elected. Sometimes they wear uniforms; sometimes they don't.

3 Sometimes a person has authority over us because they love us and we trust them **(display OHP 2)**. With people like these – perhaps our parents – we know that even if we don't want to obey, what they tell us to do is for our own good.

4 Often there are consequences if we ignore the authority of others over us **(display OHP 3).**

What's in control?

1 Show your audience a piece of wool and demonstrate how easy it is to break it.

2 Ask for a volunteer. Get them to sit on a chair. Wrap the ball of wool around them. As you do this, say to your volunteer and the audience that it's not only people who have authority over us. Unfortunately, we can end up being addicted to some things which we might think are harmless – like alcohol, cigarettes, gambling ... even spending money! These things can also have a kind of authority over us and we can discover, too late, that we are trapped by them.

3 At this point, ask the volunteer to break free from the wool. It should be impossible.

Emphasise that in a similar way, there may be things in the pupils' lives which are exercising a kind of control over them and trapping them. Leave the volunteer 'trapped' by the wool, whilst you continue ...

4 Explain that the Bible says we are all trapped by something: the wrong attitudes we have; the wrong things we do and say; the wrong thoughts we have. The Bible calls these 'sin'. At this point you could play part of the song *It's a sin* by The Pet Shop Boys and **display OHP 4** (optional). Continue by saying that 'sin' is not a new idea! **Display OHP 5**, showing the words from Romans 7:18,19. Ask pupils: *Does that ring true for you?*

Application

1 Say that one of the characteristics people most noticed about Jesus was that he had 'authority'. Even though he wasn't one of the rulers of the time, people realised that he had authority:

- in his teaching – it was powerful and people listened;
- over illnesses – people were healed, and even brought back to life;
- over nature – he calmed the storm;
- over sin and the death it leads to – he came back to life from the grave **(display OHP 6)**.

2 Turn back to the volunteeer trapped by the wool. Say that even though we can't free ourselves from things – bad habits, wrong thoughts, words and deeds ('sin') – Jesus can. He has the 'authority' to do that and only someone who is not 'trapped' can help those who are. Illustrate this last point by cutting the wool trapping the volunteer so that they are free to stand up. Ask them to return to their seat.

3 Explain that Jesus claimed to have authority over us because he is God. Comment that we naturally tend to dislike someone having authority over us, unless we know that they care about us and are acting on our behalf and for our good.

Christians believe that Jesus wants to have that kind of authority in our lives – he loves us, he knows what is best for us. So Christian believers are happy to say, 'Yes' to Jesus – setting them free from the things that 'trap' them and taking control of their lives.

25 BRING ON THE SUBSTITUTE

You will need:

- 3 juggling balls
- A foam 'custard pie' on a paper plate
- A towel
- A chocolate bar for a prize
- An assistant

aim

To illustrate the idea of substitution; to help pupils understand that Jesus was our substitute and what that means for us.

Content

1 Ask for a volunteer who can juggle and is willing to accept a challenge.

2 Tell the volunteer you would like him or her to juggle three juggling balls for one minute, perfectly. The audience will be their judge. No stopping or dropping is allowed.

3 Allow them to have several attempts at this feat. (If you find you have a volunteer who can juggle well, don't panic. One minute is quite a long time and under the pressure, they should crack!)

4 At the end of the 'failed' attempt, stand alongside your volunteer and ask the audience to give him or her a round of applause. Meanwhile your assistant should be standing behind you preparing a foam 'custard pie'. What he is doing should be obvious to the audience. You should continue by saying to the audience that the volunteer failed to achieve what was required of him or her, so they will have to receive the just reward for failure – because failure will not be tolerated! At this point, without hesitation or explanation, your assistant should take the 'custard pie' and put it in your face!

5 As you wipe your face, give the volunteer a prize (the bar of chocolate) and ask them to return to their seat.

Application

1 Explain that what they have just seen illustrates what Christians believe: no one is able to obey God perfectly in every way, or to do everything he requires of us. Deep down, if we are honest, we want to rebel and do just what we want.

2 The Bible says that we all deserve to be punished for our failure to live as God intended. We have made a mess of living in a way that's right.

3 The amazing thing that Christians believe is that God himself, in human form, took the just reward for our failure. Jesus was a kind of substitute: he took our place. But the punishment wasn't a 'custard pie', it was an agonising Roman execution – crucifixion. And the bonus for us is that we end up with the prize we don't deserve – heaven!

26 LIFE

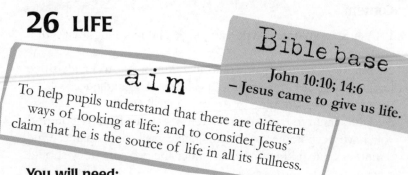

Bible base
John 10:10; 14:6
– Jesus came to give us life.

aim
To help pupils understand that there are different ways of looking at life; and to consider Jesus' claim that he is the source of life in all its fullness.

You will need:

- An OHP
- 5 OHP acetates (or 5 large cards). 4 of the OHP acetates should show the word 'life' written in 4 different ways; OHP 5 shows the word 'JESUS':

  OHP 1 – l I f e
  OHP 2 – l I F e
  OHP 3 – L i f e
  OHP 4 – L I f E
  OHP 5 – **JESUS**

Preparation

- Prepare OHP acetates as described.

Content

Introduction

Begin with a simple word association game, where two volunteers must say words associated with a given theme alternately (eg for 'holidays', your volunteers might say words like: 'sand', 'sun', 'fun' etc). As soon as one person hesitates, call up someone else to take over. Use other themes, like: 'school', 'breakfast', 'sport' etc. Then introduce the theme 'life'. They will probably find this more difficult.

Life
Comment that it's interesting how we find something we all have so difficult to describe! Say that you can think of at least four ways of describing life. Suggest that maybe they can identify with some of these ways of looking at life.

lIfe
1 Display OHP 1 which shows the word 'life' written with a capital 'I'. Say that some people spell 'life' this way. Explain that 'I', 'me' and 'my' are three of the most commonly used words in the English language. The person who sees life in this way puts him or herself first in life. They are number 1! There are things they want to do, places they want to see, money they want to make – and woe betide anyone who gets in their way! This person is a self-made man (or woman) and proud of it! They can look after themselves and don't need anyone!
2 Tell the following story:
A man was walking along a cliff. He slipped and fell and was hanging on for dear life, to a small bush, on the edge of the cliff. Although he was an atheist, he called out, in desperation, 'Is anybody there?' To his amazement, he heard a reply: 'Yes, I'm here.' He cried out again, 'What do you want me to do?' The voice said, 'Let go of the bush, and I'll save you.' He paused for a moment and then cried out, 'Is anybody else there?'*
He couldn't take the risk of trusting his life to anyone!

lIFe
1 Display OHP 2 which shows the word 'life' written with the letters 'I' and 'F' as capitals. Say that some people spell 'life' in this way – with a big 'IF' in the middle. This kind of person says things like:
  • 'If there is a God, why is there so much suffering?'
  • 'If there is a God, why did my loved one have to die?'

* This anecdote is taken from *Frogs in Cream*, Stephen Gaukroger and Nick Mercer, Scripture Union.

- 'If there is a God, why doesn't he prove it?'
- 'If I can just get through my exams, then I'll have time for God.'
- 'If God gets me that job I want, or that girl/boyfriend, then I'll believe in him.'

2 Tell this story:

Tommy was saying his prayers one night and his mum was with him. He prayed, 'Dear Lord, if you get me that mountain bike, I'll be good for a whole week.' His mum stopped him and told him that wasn't the sort of prayer God wanted to hear. 'You can't do deals with God,' she said.

Next week, he was praying again, and this time he prayed, 'Dear Lord, if you get me that mountain bike, I'll be good for two whole weeks.' His mum stopped him again and repeated the same warning.

Some time later, his mum was doing some spring cleaning. In the airing cupboard, under some towels, she found a statue of Mary. She wondered if Tommy was behind this, so she went into his room to see if she could find him. He wasn't there, but on the window-sill was a note in his handwriting which said, 'Right, God, if you ever want to see your mother again ... '!*

Life

1 **Display OHP 3** which shows the word 'life' written with the letter 'L' as a capital. Say that some people spell 'life' in this way with a capital 'L', because, after all, 'we're all learning, aren't we?' They say things like:

- 'I mean, no one's perfect are they?'
- 'We can only try our best, can't we?'

This kind of person treats life a bit like a driving test. It's as if they believe at the end of time, God will tot up the number of points they got and, hopefully, they will just about manage to scrape into heaven! But unfortunately, some of us just don't learn!

2 Tell this story:

There was a man who was doing a parachute jump. He pulled the cord – nothing happened. He pulled the emergency cord, and still nothing happened. As he was heading

---

* This anecdote is taken from *Frogs in Cream*, Stephen Gaukroger and Nick Mercer, Scripture Union.

towards earth at a hundred and twenty miles an hour, he passed another man on the way up!

'Hey!' he shouted at him, 'Do you know anything about parachutes?'

'No!' the man replied, 'Do you know anything about gas ovens?'

We're all learners!

LIfE

1 Display OHP 4 which shows the word 'life' written with the letters 'L', 'I' and 'E' as capitals. Say that some people spell 'life' in this way because, as we all know, there are many voices wanting to get our attention out there in the world, and we have to try to decide which is the truth and which are lies. Sadly, some people have ended up living their lives according to the lies they have heard and believed, like:
  * 'You're worthless, you'll never be any good.'
  * 'You've got to look good to be accepted.'
  * 'Go on, do it, everyone does it.'
  * 'Go on, take it, it won't do you any harm.'
2 Tell this story:
  There was a person who jumped out of a sixteen storey building just to see what it felt like. Half-way down, he shouted to his friends, 'See! So far so good!'

Application

1 Say that Christians aren't very good spellers, because they spell 'life' like this: JESUS (**display OHP 5** which shows the word 'Jesus'). It's not because they can't spell, but because Jesus said things like:
  * 'I am the way, the truth, and the life' (John 14:6, *Good News Bible*).
  * 'I have come ... that you might have life – life in all its fullness' (John 10:10, *Good News Bible*).
It was as if Jesus was saying, 'This is life, knowing me!' These are amazing claims that are worth checking out.
2 Conclude by challenging pupils to ask themselves : 'What am I going to base my life on?'

SECTION 4

GOD AND YOU

27 IN GOD'S IMAGE?

aim

To explore with pupils the idea of 'image', and to help them see that we are made in God's image.

You will need:

- 2 or 3 brief descriptions of pupils who will be in the assembly
- An OHP
- OHP acetates as follows:

    OHP 1 – showing a photo of yourself

    OHP 2 – showing the words, 'God created human beings in his image' (see Genesis 1:26)

    OHP 3 – showing the list of assumptions about what makes people feel valuable (see **Content** below)

    OHP 4 – showing the list of opposite assumptions (see **Content** below)

- Several pictures of a variety of famous people photocopied onto OHP acetates (optional)
- A large mirror
- 2 or 3 small prizes (eg chocolate bars)

Preparation

- In advance ask a teacher to write brief descriptions which give clues to the identity of two or three pupils who will be in the assembly.
- Prepare the OHP acetates as described.

Content

Who is it?

1 Begin by saying that you are going to describe someone who is present in the assembly. Read one clue to the person's identity at a time, eventually revealing who it is if no one guesses. Give a small prize to the one who guesses correctly. Repeat this guessing game once or twice.

2 Say that the information you have about someone builds up an 'image' of that person. The image in our mind is not the actual person, but it helps us to recognise the person.

3 Then take the mirror and let several pupils see themselves in it. It's another kind of image – visible this time, but actually, it's still not you, because it's only 2D; also it doesn't smell, and anyway, it's the wrong way round!

4 **Display OHP 1** (the picture of yourself). Say that this might be the right way round, but it still doesn't tell them everything about you, because there's more to you than your incredibly good looks! Point out that you also have: personality, opinions, a few abilities, feelings – and the picture doesn't show all of your body! (You could expand this point by showing some pictures of famous people which are easily recognisable, but still, of course, don't reveal much about the people behind the image.)

Comment that an image isn't 'the real thing', but it helps you to recognise and get to know the real thing.

Who am I?

1 Tell the pupils that the Bible has something to say about human beings and 'image'. **Display OHP 2** ('God created human beings in his image'). Say that Christians believe this is what makes human beings special and valuable.

2 Continue by saying that if you don't believe what the Bible says about our being made in God's image, you have a problem. You have to create your own 'image' based on alternative assumptions about what makes human beings valuable, for example **(display OHP 3)**:

- I wear Nike trainers, therefore I am a valuable person.
- To live is to spend.
- My jacket cost over £100, therefore I am important.
- I have lots of money, therefore I am a fulfilled human being.
- To have a high status job is to be fully alive.
- I've got ten grade A GCSEs, therefore I am someone.
- People are afraid of me, so I must be pretty cool.

Or we may see ourselves as the negatives of some of these **(display OHP 4)**:

- I wear Nick's trainers, therefore I am worthless.
- I don't have much spending money, therefore I hardly exist.

- I haven't got any GCSEs, therefore I am a nobody.
- I do not have a job, so I'm as good as dead.
- I don't have many friends, so I must be pretty worthless.

Application

1 Display OHP 2 ('God created human beings in his image') again. Say that Christians believe that this truth is what makes us special and valuable. It doesn't mean there's some big mistake, because we don't all have long beards and wear dressing gowns (like people sometimes imagine God!). Remind them that, as you have already considered, there is more to a person than looks. To be made in God's image implies something about other characteristics:

- The Bible depicts God as a person, not a thing. So we too have personality, with the capacity to feel things like love, anger and sorrow. And we are able to think, reason and argue. Mixing with other 'persons' is vital to our growth and development as people.
- Like God, we have the ability to make decisions, to choose between options, to obey or not to obey, to be cruel or to be kind – because, like God, we have free will.
- Then there is the unseen realm of the spiritual. The Bible says that 'God is Spirit' (John 4:24, *Good News Bible*). If we are made in his image, then that must be true for us too. There is something more to people than meets the eye, so that the end of our time on earth, is not the end of us. Someone once referred to the 'God-shaped vacuum' inside each human being, meaning that everyone somehow has an awareness of God. If the Bible is correct when it says we have been made in the image of God, then this is also part of how God has made us.

2 Christians believe that what makes us special is our uniqueness. Yes, that is because we all have a different look, a different 'image', a different outside; but also because we are unique in all of creation – the real me, what makes me the kind of person I am on the inside, has been made in God's image. Perhaps recognising that is an important step in becoming truly 'human'.

3 Conclude with a few moments of quiet. Ask pupils to reflect on what makes them feel special and valuable.

28 BEST OF FRIENDS

aim
To help pupils consider what makes a good friend; and to explore the idea of friendship with God.

You will need:

- A series of questions to ask two friends about each other see **Content** below)
- An OHP
- Pictures to accompany the *Hey!* * story, photocopied onto OHP acetates (illustrated)

Preparation

- Devise questions for the 'Knowing me, knowing you' game.
- Prepare acetates as illustrated.
- Find out in advance the names of two pupils who are very good friends and who are unlikely to be embarrassed at being asked to come to the front in the assembly.

Content

Knowing me, knowing you

1 Say that you would like two volunteers who are the best of friends. Then call out the two people who you have found out about in advance.

2 Interview them about how long they have known each other; what sort of things they do together; whether they have ever stopped being friends at any time etc.

OHP 1

© Brett Jordan/CPO

*The *Hey!* story and pictures are used with kind permission of Christian Publicity Organisation, Worthing Leaflet CPO735 available from CPO. See address list at back of book.

© Brett Jordan/CPO

© Brett Jordan/CPO

© Brett Jordan/CPO

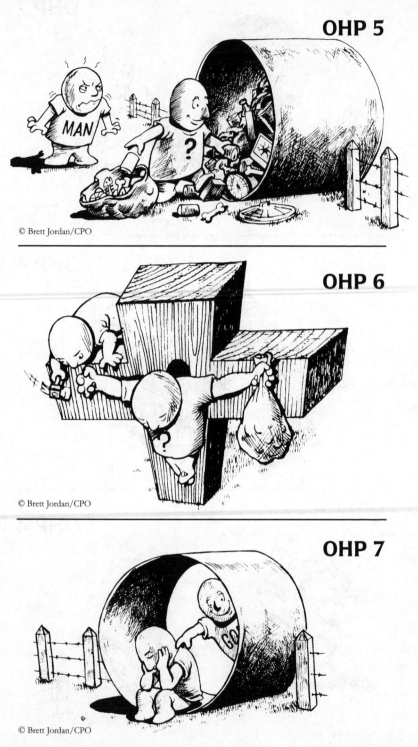

OHP 5

© Brett Jordan/CPO

OHP 6

© Brett Jordan/CPO

OHP 7

© Brett Jordan/CPO

3 Announce that they are going to take part in a game to see how well they know each other. You are going to ask one of them to leave the room while you ask the other questions about their friend.

4 When one has left the room, tell the audience that you would like them to remember the remaining friend's answers. Then ask the following multiple choice questions:

• It's break-time and your friend is feeling peckish. Would she/he prefer:
  a) a packet of crisps
  b) a crispy apple
  c) a bar of chocolate
  d) something else?

• You give your friend a birthday present but she/he doesn't like it. Would she/he:
  a) tell you 'I don't like it'
  b) pretend she/he liked it but put it away and never use it?
  c) pretend she/he liked it but take it back to the shop and change it
  d) something else?

• Has your friend got any annoying habits:
  a) picks his/her nose
  b) talks too much
  c) is always late
  d) something else?

5 Invite the friend back in and ask her/him to give her/his answers to the same questions. Encourage applause for the 'correct' answers and be generous even when they get any wrong. Ask the two friends to return to their seats.

6 Make the point that even though the contestants have done extremely well, they don't know everything about one another. How could they? In any case, if my friends knew everything about me, perhaps they wouldn't want to be my friends!

Point out that even the best of friends fall out from time to time, but it's always good to make friends again. Usually, though, it takes one person to make the first move!

Knowing God

Say that you are now going to look at the ongoing story of God's friendship with us.

Tell the *Hey!* story, displaying the pictures on OHP acetates in order as you do so.

- **Display OHP 1.** Tell the story:

  In the beginning, God and man were on very good terms. Even though God was in heaven and man was on earth, nothing got in the way of their friendship.

  > 'Hello, God,' said man.
  > 'Hello, man,' said God.

- **Display OHP 2.** Continue:

  But one day, man decided he didn't care if God was there or not. He didn't care whether he was God's friend or not. So he carelessly threw something into the tube.

  > 'Oh no!' thought God.

- **Display OHP 3.** Continue:

  Before long, the tube was full of all sorts of rubbish that came between man and God. Written on the rubbish were words like: 'pride', 'envy', 'hatred' and 'anger'. They were no longer on speaking terms and it broke God's heart. He loved man – very much. Man just stood there, proudly.

- **Display OHP 4.** Continue:

  But God wouldn't leave it that way. So, he disguised himself as a human, and climbed over onto earth, carrying a large, empty sack.

- **Display OHP 5.** Continue:

  And he began to collect together all the rubbish that was filling the tube. Man didn't like this. He didn't want this mystery man interfering in his life!

- **Display OHP 6.** Continue:

  So he murdered him. And, because the mystery man wouldn't let go of the sack, that got nailed up there with him.

- **Display OHP 7.** Continue:

  Man was feeling pretty down about everything that had happened. Something inside him was wrong. Something inside him was missing. Then, three days later, he felt a tap on his shoulder and a voice he recognised said,

  > 'Hey! How about turning around? Come on, I forgive you!
  > How about being friends again?'

Application

1 Comment that it's great to make friends again when things have got in the way of your friendship.

2 Explain that Christians believe that God is the sort of friend who never lets you down. When 'rubbish' (give examples: envy, pride etc) gets in the way of your friendship, he is always ready to forgive you – even though it's you have who let *him* down.

29 THE UNIVERSE, GOD AND ME

aim

To help pupils consider the vastness of the universe and the question of the significance of human beings.

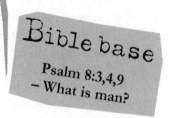

Bible base

Psalm 8:3,4,9
– What is man?

You will need:

- OHP acetates, pictures, posters or colour transparencies of the following:

    OHP/picture 1 – the sun or another nearby star

    OHP/picture 2 – a galaxy, for example, the Andromeda galaxy

    OHP/picture 3 – a cluster of galaxies, for example, the Virgo cluster

- An OHP or appropriate equipment to display the pictures
- 23 large pieces of card: the number '1' written on the first; '0' on all the others
- A beautifully wrapped gift with an accompanying card addressed, 'To someone special'

Preparation

- Prepare the pictures (OHP acetates etc). You may be able to obtain these from the school science department or astronomy club. For further information write to: Armagh Planetarium, College Hill, Armagh, Northern Ireland (phone: 01861 524725).

Content

Introduction

Begin the assembly by selecting someone from the audience and presenting them with a beautifully wrapped gift (eg a small box of chocolates). Also give them a card, the envelope of which is clearly marked, 'To someone very special'. Make sure that the audience are aware of what is happening and what the words on the envelope say.

The universe

1 Ask: *How many stars are there in the universe?* After receiving some suggestions from the pupils, say that we know about at least one star – our sun **(display OHP 1)**. Ask a pupil to come to the front to hold up the card showing the number '1'. They should stand on one side of the front area of the hall.

Explain that the sun is a huge ball of hydrogen gas, large enough for a million earths to fit inside it. Light from the sun takes eight minutes to travel the huge distance to the earth.

2 Continue by explaining that the sun is only one star in our local group of stars, which is called the Milky Way galaxy. Ask if anyone has seen the Milky Way? Say that if they can get somewhere where there are no street lights, on a clear night, they will be able to see a diffuse band of light across the sky. This is the Milky Way. Explain that it's a vast collection of stars which are like our sun. Say that if we were to take a ride in the Starship Enterprise and go out of our galaxy and look back, we would see something like this **(display OHP 2)**.

Tell pupils that our galaxy contains this many stars (ask eleven more pupils to come to the front to hold up eleven of the '0' cards. They should stand next to the pupil holding the number '1' card). Explain that this is 100 billion. Our galaxy is so vast that it is 100,000 light years across.

3 But this is only one galaxy among many! **(Display OHP 3.)** Remember, each galaxy contains about 100 billion stars. Ask how many galaxies there are in the universe? Explain that there are about 100 billion!

4 To work out how many stars there are in the universe, you need to multiply 100 billion by 100 billion and you get ... (ask eleven more pupils to come and hold up the remaining '0' cards, so that the number is stretched across the front of the assembly hall) ... a very large number indeed! This number was once likened to the number of the grains of sand on the beaches of the world (Genesis 22:17)!

5   Read Psalm 8:3,4 and 9, whilst **OHP 3** and the number are still being displayed. Then ask the pupils holding the number cards to sit down, but leave on display **OHP 3**.

Application

1   Ask pupils what they think the vast, unimaginable size of the universe means for our understanding of our own place in it.

Say that some people simply conclude that we are totally insignificant and that our existence and that of the whole universe have no purpose at all.

Christians take a different view. The Bible acknowledges that this whole universe is the creation of God. The reason it is so vast is a demonstration of the exciting and extravagant being that God is! But far from man being insignificant, God has chosen to reach out to human beings in a special way.

2   Ask pupils if they have ever had the experience of being chosen out of a vast crowd (like the person who received the gift at the beginning of the assembly), and because of that they have felt special.

3   Explain that Christians believe human beings are special, in spite of their apparent insignificance in this vast universe – because God chose to come in the person of Jesus to demonstrate his love and care for us. We might be a very small part of the universe, but we are a very special part!

4   Draw pupils' attention to the picture of the galaxies again (**OHP 3**, still on display). Say that you are going to end this assembly with a few moments of quiet. As they look at the picture, ask them to let it remind them, not of their insignificance in such a great universe, but of their *great* significance to God!

[handwritten: UNIQUE TALENT? BIRTHDAY? AWARDS CEREMONIES ⊃ SPECIAL PPL]

30 YOU'RE SPECIAL! *[handwritten: ⊃ SPECIAL PPL]*

aim

To show everyone is special to God, whatever they have done, whoever they are and whatever they possess.

[handwritten: What Makes someone special?]

You will need:

- A prize (eg a chocolate bar)

Preparation

- Prepare a list for the 'Sit down if … ' game.
- Rehearse your reading or recitation of the poem.

Content

Sit down if …

1 Ask everyone to stand up and follow your instructions very carefully. Say that they are only to sit down when you say something that applies to them. Each instruction you give will begin with the words, 'Sit down if … ' Here are some ideas you could use. Devise some more of your own in case you need them.

- There is a Cliff Richard album in your house.
- You have owned a hamster at some point in your life.
- You have been to Spain on holiday.
- You've got blue eyes.
- You play a musical instrument.
- Your front door is red.
- You have a CD-Rom at home.
- You have never seen a single episode of *Neighbours*.

2 When most people have sat down and there are just two or three people left standing, you will probably need to choose something which you can see separates them (eg 'Sit down if you have red hair'), in order to get down to one person.

3 Bring 'the winner' to the front. Go over all the things you have discovered about this person – all the things they've managed to avoid (a Cliff Richard album etc).

4 Ask them how it feels to be so special. Out of all these people, only *they* have this unique combination of characteristics – the only one in this year (this school etc)!

Award the person a prize and ask the audience to give them a round of applause.

Everyone is special!

1 Then ask what would have happened if you had asked different questions. Make the point that you would have had different people sitting and standing and a different person out at the front as 'the winner'! In fact, you could probably have 'arranged' it so that any one person there could be the 'special' one brought out to the front. Everyone is special!

2 Say that you hope they have been told before, 'You're special!' But, it's not what we've done or possess or have had in the past that makes us special. Our uniqueness is more than being the only person never to have watched a single edition of *Neighbours*, or the only person with that special brand of trainers, or the only person to have been to Florida a dozen times! No, God says each of us is special for other reasons.

3 Read this poem:

In all the world there is nobody like you.
Since the beginning of time, there has never been another
    person like you,
Nobody has your smile, your eyes, your hands, your hair.
Nobody owns your handwriting, your voice.
You're special.
Nobody can paint your brush strokes.
Nobody has your taste for food or music or dance or art.
Nobody in the universe sees things as you do.
In all time there has never been anybody who laughs in
    exactly your way,
And what makes you laugh or cry or think
May cause a totally different response in another,
So ... you're special.
You are different from any other person who has ever lived
    in all history.
You are the only one in the whole of creation
Who has your particular set of abilities.
There is always someone who is better at one thing or
    another than you,
But no one has your combination of talents and feelings.

Through all eternity, no one will ever walk, talk, think,
Or do anything exactly like you.
You're special.
You're rare, and in all rarity there is enormous value
And because of your great value,
The need for you to imitate anyone else is absolutely
    unnecessary.
You're special ... and it's no accident you are.
Please realise God made you for a special purpose.
He has a job for you to do as well as you can.
Out of the billions of applicants, only one is qualified.
Only one has the unique and right combination of what it
    takes,
And that one is you.*

4 Sit down with no further comment.

---

* Source unknown.

31 IT COULD BE YOU!

aim

To help pupils reflect on what they can be sure of in life; and to help them understand that they can depend on God.

You will need:

- Several ten pence coins
- A supply of small chocolate bars (eg *Chomps*)
- 2 large dice made out of sponge
- A national lottery ticket
- An OHP
- 2 OHP acetates prepared as follows:
  OHP 1 – showing the National Lottery logo: 'It could be you!' (words and picture)
  OHP 2 – showing two large numbers: '1' followed by 17 '0's; '1' followed by 57 '0's
- 2 pieces of paper, with the message, 'Congratulations!' written on them

Preparation

- Prepare the OHP acetates as described.
- Before pupils enter the assembly hall, stick the 'Congratulations!' messages underneath two of the chairs.
- Find out how many pupils there will be approximately in the assembly, so that you can work out 'the odds' in advance (see **Content** below).

Content

It could be you

1 Display OHP 1. Begin by saying that this morning (in this assembly etc), 'It could be you!' Say that you are going to walk through the audience, offering people a 1 in 2 chance of winning. You will toss a coin and if the person you ask guesses correctly, heads or tails, they win the ten pence piece!

2 Do this until you have lost three or four coins, just to show you are genuine!

3 Comment that already there have been some lucky winners. But to be honest, there was a good chance of winning. A 1 in 2 chance!

4 Say that now you are going to make it harder. In this room of perhaps 300 people (use the appropriate number) there will be just two lucky winners of the next prize. That is a 1 in 150 chance of winning. Tell pupils to feel under their chairs for the hidden message. The two winners come to the front (applause), and receive their prizes of ten pence each. But then offer them an opportunity to increase their winnings.

5 At this point, bring out the dice. Ask if anyone can tell you the most common score you get when you throw two dice. The answer is seven. You have a 1 in 6 chance of getting that.

6 Offer the two contestants £10 for their 10p piece if they can achieve a score of seven, three times on the run.

7 Let each contestant have a turn, but they will fail – because the actual chance of doing it three times in a row is 1 in 216. Ask the audience to give them a round of applause. Give them each a *Chomp*, but tell them that gambling is a mug's game. There was no way they could win and that you, the 'bookmaker', would always eventually come out on top!

Life's a lottery

1 Comment that, inspite of the unlikelihood of winning, the thought that, 'It could be you!' has gripped the nation and stirred millions of people to carry on buying a lottery ticket every week.

2 Say that from its beginning, the lottery has been surrounded by controversy: one family left the country because it was against their religion to play the lottery; one man killed himself because he forgot to buy what would have been the winning ticket; shop-keepers were prosecuted for trying to fiddle the scratch card game.

3 Tell the pupils about one group of people who formed a syndicate and won £10. So, they bought ten scratch cards and won £4. Then they bought four scratch cards and won £2. So, they bought two scratch cards and didn't win anything! This is just one example of what millions of people are doing every week.

4 Some facts about the National Lottery:

• In its first year, 4½ billion pounds were spent on the lottery by the British public. That's the same amount as the GNP (all the money earned) of a country like Ethiopia. It could build ten new hospitals or four space shuttle craft.

• 75% of us play every week and ½ million people spend £20 a week on the lottery.

• More people take part in the lottery each week than have ever bothered to vote in any general election.

• More money is spent on the lottery per head of the population than is spent on bread.

• 150 new millionaires were created in the first year.

5 Ask pupils what they think the chance is of winning a million pounds. Show them the lottery ticket and say that no one can say they don't know the likelihood of winning, because it's printed on the ticket. You have:

• a 1 in 57 chance of winning £10;

• a 1 in 1000 (perhaps the number of pupils in school) chance of winning £65;

• a 1 in 55,500 (the biggest crowd possible at the new Old Trafford – use a local example) chance of winning £1500;

• a 1 in 2 million (five cities the size of Liverpool – use a local example) chance of winning £100,000;

• a 1 in 14 million chance of winning 'the big one'.

6 Say that you can tell them with some confidence that they are not going to win 'the big one', unless they use the guaranteed method. Theoretically, to be absolutely sure of winning, all you have to do is spend £10 a week for the next 28,000 years – then you will be sure to win!

Against the odds

Say that you want to tell them about someone who did something against all the odds:

• His birth, life, and death were all predicted in considerable detail. There were 300 predictions about him altogether and hundreds of years later he lived out each one. His name was Jesus.

• It had been predicted where he would be born, that he would be betrayed by his friends, die by crucifixion, be a poor man, but be buried in a rich man's tomb. 300 predictions in all.

• A professor of mathematics and astronomy did some research. He took just eight of the 300 predictions and asked 'What is the chance of these predictions being fufilled by any one man?' And he discovered the chance was 1 in ... (**display OHP 2**, revealing the first number, but keeping the second number covered). That's more people than have ever lived!

• Then the professor took forty-eight of the 300 predictions and asked what the chance was of them being fulfilled by any one man and he found the answer to be one in ... (uncover the second number on **OHP 2**).

Application

1 In a world where all of life seems a bit like a lottery and you can't be sure of anything or anyone, it's tempting to rely on luck in to bring us some happiness and security.

2 So is there anything we *can* be sure of?

• Well, we are all going to die. You have a 1 in 1 chance of dying.

• But Christians also believe you can be sure of God. He is totally reliable and worth listening to. What he says *is* going to happen. He is the only 'dead cert'.

3 **Display OHP 1** again as a focus for pupils as you finish the assembly.

32 THAT'S IMPOSSIBLE!

You will need:

- Plenty of sheets of A4 paper
- An OHP, OHP acetates and pens
- Chocolate bars as prizes

aim

To show that God has done the impossible – made it possible for us to be his friends!

Preparation

- Practice 'the impossible tear' (see illustration) and 'the impossible paper folding' exercises. Memorise and practice making 'the impossible cross' (see illustration), until you can do it without looking at the instructions or making a mistake.
- 'The impossible task' (see illustration): you could copy this onto OHP acetates in advance. Or, if you prefer you could draw on an OHP acetate as you are speaking, adding the different elements of the illustration as you talk. If you choose to do this, practice in advance.

Content

Explain that during this assembly you are going to ask for several volunteers, who need to be prepared to attempt an 'impossible' task.

The impossible tear!

1 Tell the volunteer that their task is to tear a piece of A4 paper into three pieces. Give the volunteer the sheet of paper, which you have prepared in advance with two tears already in place (see illustration).

THE IMPOSSIBLE TEAR

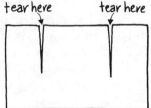

2 The volunteer must hold the two ends of the paper, and in one action, tear it into three pieces. It's impossible! Allow two or three volunteers to attempt this.

3 Eventually, demonstrate it yourself by holding the middle section of the paper between your teeth or lips, and pulling the ends away from you with your hands. You'll find it is possible after all! Give the volunteers a round of applause and a prize each.

The impossible paper-folding task

Ask the next volunteer to fold a piece of A4 paper in half, eight times. It's impossible! Even you won't be able to do it! Give your volunteer a round of applause and a prize.

The impossible cross

Tell the volunteer that they have to make a cross out of a sheet of A4 paper with only one straight tear. Let them have several attempts. Eventually, show how it's done, using the method illustrated.

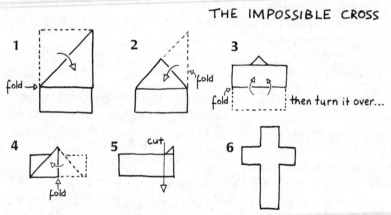

THE IMPOSSIBLE CROSS

The impossible intelligence test

Ask for a volunteer who doesn't mind taking an intelligence test. He or she must answer all the following questions correctly:

- How many animals of each species did Moses take on board the Ark? (Answer: *None. It wasn't Moses, it was Noah!*)
- Which country has a 4th July – the UK or the USA? (Answer: *They both do!*)
- What is the next letter in this sequence: O T T F F S S ? (Answer: *'E'. They are the first letters of numbers, starting at 'one'.*)
- If you take two apples from three apples, how many have you got? (Answer: *Two – because you have taken two!*)

The volunteer will have done very well if he/she gets them all correct. Give them a round of applause and a prize.

The impossible task

1 Refer back to the to 'the impossible tear', 'the impossible paper-folding', 'the impossible cross' and 'the impossible intelligence test'. Comment how some things really *are* impossible, some things just *seem* to be impossible and some things are *just about* possible.

2 Explain that in one way the Bible is all about how God accomplished an impossible task: how he – a holy, pure God – found a way to make friends with humans, who had turned their backs on him and gone their own way, doing what was evil. In fact, man had turned away from God to such an extent that there was a huge gulf separating humans from God (**display or draw diagram 1** on the OHP).

3 God seemed a million miles away and despite the fact that humans tried to reach God (**display/ draw diagram 2**), the gulf remained. How could they bridge the gulf?

4 What was impossible for human beings, was possible for God – but only by becoming himself, in human form, the bridge. By dying on the cross, Jesus was able to do the impossible, by becoming the bridge between man and God. (**Display/draw diagram 3**; or, you could use the paper cross you made earlier, placed on the OHP, but check this will work in advance.)

THE IMPOSSIBLE TASK

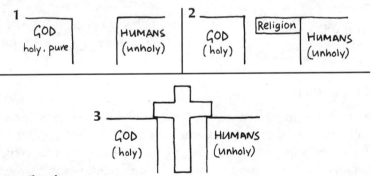

Application

1 Talk briefly about the Indiana Jones film, *The Last Crusade*. Mention the part where Indiana Jones is standing with his back up against the wall, with a huge chasm in front of him which he must get across. To help him, all he has in his hand is his father's guide book. 'There's no way I can jump this,' he says, 'It's impossible!'

Then, looking in the book, he sees that it describes an invisible bridge and he realises, 'It's a step of faith!' So, hesitatingly he steps out (you could demonstrate his actions). To his surprise, his foot lands on solid rock – the bridge! He wasn't absolutely sure that there *was* a bridge, but it said there was in the book that he trusted – and there was!

2   Say that Christians all around the world – and throughout the centuries since Jesus – have taken a similar step of faith. They have discovered that God can do the impossible; instead of seeming a million miles away, God has become the closest friend they have. But for this to happen, we've got to use the 'bridge' God provided (point to diagram 3). Jesus' death on the cross is what made it possible for us to be friends with God.

33 IT'S GOOD TO TALK

aim

To help pupils understand that prayer is part of a relationship with God.

Bible base

Luke 18:9-14 – the parable of the Pharisee and the tax collector.

You will need:

• A mobile phone

Preparation

• Arrange, in advance, for someone to be waiting for a phone call from you during the assembly. It could be your mother or father or someone posing as them. Alternatively, you could arrange for the person to phone you during the assembly (when you are ready, dial the number you want and let it ring a couple of times as a signal to the person to ring you back).

• Rehearse the phone conversation in advance, along the lines indicated in the **Content** section below.

• Rehearse your reading or telling of the story of the Pharisee and the tax collector (Luke 18:9-14).

Content

Phone home!

1 Begin by saying that you have got your mobile phone with you this morning (show it to the pupils). Comment how amazing it is that you can speak to anyone you like, as long as they are near a phone, within a few seconds. How is that possible? There are so many messages rushing around the earth. This phone is not even connected by wires or cables! The technology is incredible!

2 Mention that you were told that 'orange' ones were good, but the shop only had black ones in stock!

3 Suggest that you could make a call, here and now, from the assembly! Explain that you know someone who is in, because you always have a chat on the phone at this time of day. Tell everyone that it's your mother or father (don't say the number!). Say that everyone will have a chance to talk to him or her. Ask the audience to keep very quiet until you give a signal and then they must shout, 'Hiya Mum (Dad).' Give the audience a practice at doing this before you phone.

4 Make the call and during the (pre-arranged) conversation, make sure you include the following:

- say thank you for something;
- say sorry about something;
- ask for a favour;
- make it appear that you are listening to some advice (eg by saying something like, 'OK I will');
- end by saying, 'I love you' so softly that you have to repeat it, to your 'embarrassment'! Let everyone say 'Hiya Mum (Dad)!' and end the call.

5 Comment that your mobile phone is a good one but it's got its limitations. For example, you have to keep it turned on and the batteries fade; it has to be within range and, as with any phone, the person you are trying to call has to be in and has to want to talk to you! Say that you doubt whether you could talk to the Queen, although there was a Canadian journalist who once managed it!

Talk with God

1 Explain that you have another mobile phone that's usable any time and at any range. It has free rental and there are no charges for calls. It's called 'prayer'. Christians think of prayer as being like a two-way conversation, a bit like using the phone. Then add that they may have noticed, though, how some people treat phones as though they are made for one-way conversations! They forget that there are two parts to a phone. Ask if they have ever had that sort of experience? (Hold the phone, outstretched, away from your ear!)

2 Comment that some people treat prayer like that, too. They keep on talking *at* God, instead of having a conversation *with* him.

3 Read or tell the story of the Pharisee and the tax collector (Luke 18:9-14) from a contemporary version of the Bible.

Application

1 Make the point that although we may not feel good enough to pray, that is the very attitude God is looking for in prayers! Instead of long, formal prayers, the Bible shows people talking to God as a person – which is what he is!

2 Remind everyone that during your telephone call earlier, there were three very important things you said: there was a 'thank you', a 'sorry' and 'a please'. And those are exactly the sort of things that many Christians try to include in their prayers with God: telling him about all the things that have happened to them and are going to happen; all the different ways in which they have felt, happy, angry, disappointed.

Conversation with God – prayer – is about being real with someone who is always at the end of the line, never out, never switched off, and who never has flat batteries!

3 The conversation you had on the phone earlier also included your listening to some advice and being reminded of some things you had forgotten. And there was also a chance to say how you felt about your mum (dad). For the Christian, these things are part of prayer too.

4 Conclude by reminding everyone that conversation is part of a relationship; and prayer is part of our relationship with God. Like all relationships, it needs working at! Encourage pupils to talk with God. It's good to talk.

THROUGH THE YEAR

Harvest
Christmas
St Valentine's Day
Easter
Work experience

HARVEST

34 HOW DO YOU SPELL HARVEST?

aim

To encourage pupils to be ready
to share with those in need.

Bible base
Luke 16:19-31
– the rich man and
Lazarus.

You will need:

- 7 pieces of card, each one showing a letter of the word 'harvest'
- Some unusual fruit (eg a star fruit, a fig, a kiwi fruit, a mango, an avocado; a toffee apple – for fun!)
- A diagram of 'the global village'* (see illustration) copied onto a large piece of card or OHP acetate
- 6 jam-filled, sugar-coated doughnuts
- A roll of kitchen towel

4140 PEOPLE

- **1 in 5 will die before 20.**
- **1 in 10 chance of seeing a health worker in their life.**
- **Spend less than 2 years at school.**

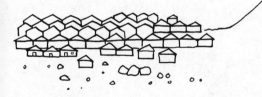

860 PEOPLE

- **80% of the baths**
- **75% of the cars**
- **½ of all the money**
- **8 times more doctors**
- **25 times the wages**

---

* This illustration is adapted from material in *God, Justice and Power*, Scripture Union and TEAR Australia.

Preparation

- Prepare cards showing the letters to make the word 'harvest'.
- Prepare the diagram of 'the global village' as illustrated.

Content

Introduction

1 Begin by saying that you are going to be thinking about the meaning of harvest time in this assembly.

2 Ask for seven volunteers. Give each of them one of the cards showing a letter from the word 'harvest'. Ask them to order themselves, so that the letters spell the word 'harvest'.

Harvest time is about ...

- **EARTH**

1 Ask the volunteers to order themselves so that the letters spell 'earth'.

2 Say that harvest time is about celebrating all the good things the earth provides. Remind pupils that there is produce in our shops from all over the world. Some of it is familiar, some less so.

3 Show pupils the pieces of 'unusual' fruit, one at a time. Ask them if anyone can tell you what each is called. If the person you ask gets the answer correct, give them the piece of fruit. (Show them a toffee apple for fun!)

4 Comment that the variety of food in the world is staggering. And there is so much of it – enough to feed twice the world's population. And all this is what is remembered at harvest time – as a gift from God.

- **STARVE**

1 Ask the volunteers to rearrange themselves, so that the letters spell the word 'starve'.

2 Say that in spite of the vast supplies of food on our planet, people are starving – not just a few people tucked away in the corner of the world, but millions of people!

3 Say that if this world of 5.7 billion people were described as if it were a global village of 5000 people, we would discover some interesting facts. (**Display the diagram of 'the global village'.**) Talk about the contrasts which exist between the lives of the rich and the poor.

4 Comment that the world's resources are not evenly spread. Ask: *How can this be put right?*

- SHARE

1 Ask the volunteers to order themselves so that the letters spell the word 'share'.

2 Announce that you could all 'share' now! Ask who would like a doughnut. Ask for three more volunteers.

3 Give each volunteer a doughnut and give them this instruction: This doughnut must be eaten, but you must not lick your lips!

4 Tell the audience you would like them to help with this challenge by shouting, 'Licking your lips!' if they spot anyone doing just that. Have the kitchen towel handy!

5 Allow about thirty seconds for the challenge. At the end of the ensuing mayhem, see who has eaten the most without licking their lips.

6 Then remind them that the instruction was that the doughnut must be eaten, but that they must not lick their lips! Ask how else they could have achieved the task. Eventually someone will realise that it could be done by feeding someone else!

7 Then give each of the three volunteers another doughnut and ask them to go and feed as many people as possible!

8 After a few moments ask them to return to their seats and give them a round of applause.

- HEART

1 Ask the audience what they think will have to happen for people to be willing to share on a global – or even local – scale.

2 Say that the final word you want your volunteers to spell is 'heart'. Ask the volunteers to order themselves so that the letters spell the word 'heart'.

3 Say that for people to be willing to share so that everyone in the world has all they need, there needs to be a change of heart – starting with you and me. It has been said that we need to live more simply, so that others may simply live!

Application

1 Tell the story which Jesus told about the rich man and the poor man called Lazarus (Luke 16:19-31). Lazarus sat each day at the gate of the rich man, begging. In the story, they both died. The poor man went to heaven and the rich man went to hell. The point of the story wasn't that the rich man was to blame for the poor man's state, but that he ignored him and did nothing to help.

2 Comment that it's easy to think that we can't do anything. After all, the poor and the starving are too far away for us to be able to make any difference, aren't they? But we *can* do something: we can give our money to those working to relieve hunger; and we can ask God to change our hearts – now, today, so that we are more willing to share with those around us here.

CHRISTMAS

35 IT'S CHRISTMAS!

> ### aim
> To remind pupils that amidst all the excitement and chaos of Christmas, we need to take time to receive God's gift to us – Jesus.

You will need:

* For the gift-wrapping game: Christmas wrapping paper; ribbon and bows; 3 sealed cardboard boxes; 3 rolls of sellotape; 3 pairs of scissors; and 3 tables for participants to work on.
* Chocolate bars for prizes
* A clean dustbin containing: used Christmas paper; tinsel; Christmas cards; a half-eaten sandwich and mince pie; empty alcohol bottles; a Christmas record or tape; a gaudy tie; a tangerine; a party popper; a broken toy; and a beautifully wrapped 'gift', decorated with bows and ribbon.

Preparation

* Before the pupils enter the assembly hall, set up three tables and place on each a set of equipment for the gift-wrapping game.
* Prepare the dustbin in advance and place it ready for when you need it during the assembly.
* Prepare the 'beautifully wrapped gift' in advance. The 'gift' is a box with the following written on three of the sides: 'Emmanuel'; 'God with us'; 'Jesus'.

Content

Before ...

1 Talk about pupils' preparations for Christmas. Ask: *Has anyone has sent some cards yet? Has anyone bought all their presents yet? Has anyone started wrapping presents?* Say that in this assembly you're going to recreate a scene typical in many households at the moment.

2 Ask for three volunteers and tell them you would like each of them to stand behind one of the tables. Explain that they have to wrap the small box they have in front of them, as neatly and quickly as possible. Go through all the equipment laid on the table in front of them, which they are to use. Then give them the opportunity to invite a friend to come and help them with the sellotape etc. Make sure that the audience can see what is happening.

3 Set a time limit (eg sixty seconds) and play some well-known Christmas music whilst the participants are working. Stop the music at the end of the time limit and have a look at what they have managed to achieve. Give them a round of applause and a prize each.

After ...

1 Comment that Christmas is often like that. All the preparation for months, the excitement and chaos – then, suddenly it's all over. It's a bit of an anti-climax really.

2 Ask: *And what are we left with after Christmas?* Tell pupils that you just happen to have with you a dustbin, full of the sort of things you might find in it, after Christmas. Ask them what they think a visitor from another planet who came and looked in their bins after Christmas would make of what was there.

3 Drag on the dustbin and start to take out the contents as outlined below, sometimes commenting on an item. Use the suggestions given here or devise your own:

  • The wrapping paper and tinsel.

  • The Christmas cards. Ask: Did you know that eight or nine out of ten Christmas cards have snowy Christmas scenes, cartoon creatures around a tree or a Father Christmas on the front? Point out that that only leaves one or two out of ten which have the real Christmas message on the front!

  • The party popper. Surprise the audience by letting it off.

  • The tie. Tell the story of the woman who gave her husband two ties for Christmas. He thought he'd please her by wearing one on Christmas morning. When he came downstairs, she snapped, 'What's wrong with the other one?' Comment that you just can't please some people!

- The half-eaten mince pie and sandwich. Take a bite and say, 'Turkey again!'
- A Christmas tape or CD. Say that every family has their favourite, don't they? Get them to join in singing a Christmas song (eg 'I'm dreaming of a white Christmas').
- The tangerine. Explain that for some reason, all children used to get one of these in their stockings many years ago.
- The empty bottles. Ask how many of these they think there will be this Christmas. How much misery, rows and fights will result from them? How many deaths will there be on the road this Christmas, because too many people abuse this stuff?
- The broken toy. Say that this sums up Christmas for many people. They have very high expectations which are not realised. By Boxing Day they are feeling let down, like a toy that's been broken.

4 Look as if you think the dustbin is empty, but then say something like, 'Hang on, what's this?' Acting as if you are very surprised, and reaching down to the bottom of the bin, lift out the beautifully wrapped present. Ask the pupils why they think anyone would leave a present unopened at Christmas and then put it in the bin? Comment that everyone knows that presents are to be opened and enjoyed.

5 Take the wrappings, ribbon and bows off to reveal the box beneath and the words written on three sides: 'Emmanuel'; 'God with us'; 'Jesus'.

Application

1 Show the 'gift' to everyone and say that this – the greatest present of all – will remain unopened by most people this Christmas. Comment how strange it is that the very person we remember in the story of the Nativity and for whom there was no room in the stable in Bethlehem, the very person after whom all our festivities are named, is still left outside most people's homes.

2 Say that gifts are meant to be received, opened and enjoyed (not forgetting, of course, to thank the giver).

3 Challenge pupils about how they will respond to God's gift to them this Christmas.

ST VALENTINE'S DAY

36 LOVE

aim

To show pupils that there are different kinds of love; and to help them understand the extent of God's love.

Bible base
Mark 12:29-31;
Luke 15:11-32;
1 Corinthians 13:4-7
– love.

You will need:

- A selection of funny St Valentine's day cards (but make sure you haven't missed any 'double meanings' – teenagers won't!)
- Examples from newspapers of St Valentine's day messages
- 1 Corinthians 13:4-7 copied onto an OHP acetate (use a modern Bible version)
- A jigsaw made from large pieces of card or an OHP acetate which has been cut in four, each piece showing one of 'the four loves': *storge, philia, eros* and *agape* (see illustration)

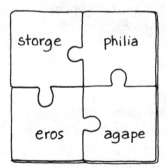

Preparation

- Prepare OHP acetates as described.
- Find out in advance from a teacher at the school if there is a widely known boy/girl relationship which the parties involved wouldn't mind being mentioned in the assembly.

Content

St Valentine's day

1 Explain that St Valentine's day is named after Valentine, a priest, who fell in love with an executioner's daughter. Sadly, the girl was blind, but the priest miraculously restored her sight. However the emperor was displeased with him. He ordered him to be clubbed to death and then his head was chopped off!

2 Over the years it became the tradition for people to remember St Valentine and his love. Gradually it became known as the day when birds choose their mates; and then people started sending the one they loved a card.

3 Show and read out some of the St Valentine's day cards. Then say that you have somehow managed to intercept one, sent by a boy who is present in this assembly to a girl who is here too. Read the message, inserting the names of the boy and girl (who you found out about in advance) in the appropriate places.

4 Point out that simply by the law of averages, you are far more likely to fall for a person, than that person is to fall for you. So, some people play safe and send their messages anonymously, sometimes through a newspaper. Read out some of the messages from newspapers that you have brought with you.

5 Say that another thing people think about on St Valentine's day is kissing! Comment that you need to be careful when kissing. Ask your audience if they know these interesting facts. When you kiss:

- you are using twenty-nine facial muscles;
- your heartbeat increases from seventy-two to ninety-five beats per minute;
- consequently the blood in your body races around a lot faster, so you feel warmer and your face goes redder and your lips enlarge;
- you may burn up three calories and ...
- some experts say your lifespan could be reduced by up to three minutes!

St Valentine's day could damage your health! Comment that perhaps it's easier to describe a kiss simply as the shortest distance between two people!

Love

1 Comment that all this talk of romance and kissing could lead you to think that that's all there is to love. Certainly the media seem to concentrate on these aspects of love. But there is more to love than just these things.

2 Jesus said that the two greatest commandments were to love God with all your strength, and to love your neighbour as yourself (see Mark 12:29-31). And St Paul (who wrote a lot of what we call the Bible) said this about love ... (**Display 1 Corinthians 13:4-7**, written on OHP acetate.) Ask pupils: *Do you think that this is a good description of the way you love others?*

3 Explain that the English language has only one word for something which the ancient Greeks had four words for! If you say in English that you 'love' someone, it immediately has certain implications that may not have been intended. But the Greeks could express themselves rather more freely. The words they could use were:

- *Storge*

This word, *storge* (**display on OHP the appropriate piece of the jigsaw**), meant 'affection'. It's the word you might use when you say 'I love fish and chips', or 'I love Llandudno', or even, 'I love old Mrs Jenkins, next door'. 'Love' used in this way doesn't mean that you want to elope with Mrs Jenkins; it means you have a deep affection for her.

- *Philia*

The second word the Greeks had was philia (**display this next piece of the jigsaw**). This word would be used to describe the feelings you have in a close friendship. It could be brotherly or sisterly love, where you have things in common with that person or are able to confide in them. It's the kind of love you might feel for a best friend. It's important that we are able to recognise this kind of love for one another, without it having any romantic associations.

- *Eros*

The third word is eros (**display this piece of the jigsaw**). It's the same word as the name of the little character in Piccadilly Circus, London, who fires an arrow from his bow and which appears on lots of St Valentine's day cards. From this word we get the English word, 'erotic'.

This kind of love means the physical attraction that St Valentine's day is about. It's to do with the kind of feeling that makes us blush or sends shivers down our spine. It's the sort of love that is portrayed in so many films and songs. It's the sort of love that may lead two people to say, 'I can't live without you. Let's get married.'

- *Agape*

The ancient Greeks' fourth word for love was agape (**put the last piece of the jigsaw in place**). The literal meaning of this word is 'sacrificial love'. It's the sort of love shown when someone gives their life to save another. It's the sort of 'mad' love that keeps on loving even when it gets nothing back in return. It's the sort of love that welcomes back an undeserving prodigal son (explain as appropriate; see Luke 15:11-32). And every time, in the New Testament, when the love of God or Jesus is mentioned, this word – *agape* – is used.

Explain that the greatest act of love, according to the Bible, is Jesus' death on the cross for the sake of people who had rejected him. In response to the question, 'How much does God love us?' some people have stretched out their arms (demonstrate this as a reminder of the crucifixion) and said, 'This much.'

Application

1 Say that it's the greatest thing in the world to know that you are loved. For many Christians the realisation that God loves them with this *agape* love – which meant Jesus dying on the cross for them – was the thing which made them want to get to know God themselves and to 'love' him in return.

2 Comment that there is a lot being said about the subject of 'love' at the present time. Say that you are going to finish the assembly with a few moments of quiet. Ask pupils to use this time to think about all the people, places and things that they could say they 'love'. If they would like to, they could take this opportunity, as they think about them, to say 'thank you' to God for them.

EASTER

37 HIDDEN MEANINGS

aim
To explore the meaning of the cross with pupils.

You will need:

- An OHP
- The following copied onto OHP acetates (or card):
  2 parking signs as illustrated
  The 'Missing the Point' drawings (see illustrations)
  'Dingbat' puzzles (see illustration)
  4 drawings showing different meanings of a cross (see illustrations)
- Several chocolate bars for prizes

Preparation

- Copy the drawings onto OHP acetates (or card) as described.
- Rehearse using the OHP acetates (or illustrations on card).

Content

Hidden meanings

1 Display the first parking sign ('Parking limited to 1 hour'). Comment that this is not too difficult to understand. **Display the second parking sign** ('Return prohibited within 1 hour'). What do they think this means? Like some people, they may not be quite so sure!

Illustrate this by telling pupils about someone who was very confused by a notice like this. He only wanted to pop to the shops for ten minutes, but because of the sign, he hung around in the shops until his time was up, so as not to break the rules! He had misunderstood the sign. He had the wrong interpretation.

And sometimes we may need to look more deeply at things than we're used to, to find out their true meaning.

2 Say that sometimes the meaning of something can be so obvious, it's staring us in the face, but we still miss the point completely! **Display the 'missing the point' drawings**, giving your audience time to take in the sense of each.

CHEEKKEECH

(cheek to cheek)

♡SIGHT   SIGHT

(love at first sight)

WORLD

(travel around the world)

111 Another Another
111 Another Another
111 Another Another

(6 of 1 and ½ dozen of another)

$\dfrac{Knee}{lights}$ (neon lights)

$\dfrac{Put}{kilogram}$ (put on weight)

ON
LAP LAP LAP (on the last lap)

135

3 Ask for four volunteers to make two teams of two people. You are going to show them some 'dingbats'. They must work out the hidden meanings. Explain that these 'dingbats' contain well-known phrases or sayings, but they will have to look carefully in order to find them. **Display the 'dingbats'** on the OHP. Award points, prizes and applause to the volunteers.

Make the point that the real meaning of some things are not always obvious at first glance.

Crosses

1 Display the drawing of Jesus' cross on OHP acetate (or card). Ask some questions about its significance. For example:
- What does this mean?
- Why is it so important to Christians?
- Why do some people hang one of these around their necks?
- Why are graveyards full of them?
- Why are some big churches built in the shape of a cross?

2 Display the drawing of an 'X' used to mark a sum wrong. Explain that one meaning of a cross can be that you have done wrong. You haven't followed the rules.

3 Display the drawing of an 'X' meant as a 'kiss' on a card. Say that a cross can also mean 'I love you.'

4 Display the drawing of Jesus' cross again. Explain that for Christians, the cross at Easter means both these things. Jesus' death on the cross was the way God dealt with all the wrong in the world – and in me. The cross also shows us how much God loves us – in Jesus he was prepared to come and die for us. (Talk about these two aspects of the meaning of the cross briefly, but as you feel appropriate, to help pupils understand the significance of the cross.)

Application

1 Display the 'crossroads' sign. Comment that the cross of Jesus also gives everyone a choice: to go God's way or our own. Explain that Christians are people who have decided to live God's way – saying 'No' to what's wrong and 'Yes' to God's love.

2 Challenge pupils to spend time this Easter thinking about the meaning of 'the cross' for them. The cross isn't meant to have a hidden meaning, but it *is* easy to miss the point!

38 ENIGMAS

aim

To show pupils that the only reasonable explanation of the mystery of the empty tomb is that Jesus rose from the dead.

Bible base

John 19 – the death and burial of Jesus;
John 20:1-10; Luke 24:1-12; Matthew 28:1-15
– the empty tomb;
John 20:11-29, 21:1-22; Luke 24:13-53; Matthew 28:16-20
– appearances of Jesus after his resurrection.

You will need:

• An OHP and OHP acetates to show the five 'enigmas' (see **Content** below)

Preparation

• Prepare the OHP acetates in advance, writing each enigma on a separate acetate.

Content

Enigmas

1 Explain that you are going to play 'enigmas'. An enigma is another name for a puzzle or a riddle. You are going to describe some situations. The contestants have to work out how and why those situations have come about. For the sake of time in this assembly, they may only ask a maximum of three questions to which you can answer 'yes' or 'no'.

2 Ask for six volunteers to make two teams of three people each. Each team takes turns in trying to solve the following 'enigmas'. **Display each 'enigma'** on the **OHP** in turn, so that everyone in the audience has the opportunity to consider them. Here are the 'enigmas' (NB: they are quite well known situations, so be prepared for quick answers!):

• In the middle of a field is a hat, a scarf, a pipe, a carrot and a few lumps of coal.
(Answer: *A snowman has melted.*)

• A man goes into a pub and asks for a glass of water. The man behind the bar takes out a gun and points it at the man's

head. The man says, 'Thanks,' and walks out. Why?
(Answer: *He had hiccups! The barman frightened him to make the hiccups stop.*)

• A man is pushing a car along. He can see a hotel in the distance and he knows that when he gets there, he'll have to give the owner of the hotel a lot of money. Why?
(Answer: *He's playing Monopoly!*)

• An empty ship is floating in calm waters. It is far from any port and is in no danger of sinking. There is no one on board, there are no signs of a struggle and it hasn't been reported missing. Why? (Answer: *It's a plastic toy boat in someone's bath!*)

3 Whether the two teams get the answers right or not, give them all a round of applause and then pose the next situation to the entire audience:

• A cave hollowed out of a rock has been used as a grave. The mystery is – it's empty. Inside, the sheets which had been wrapped around the body are lying on the floor. Why?

4 Suggest a few questions people might ask in order to solve this 'enigma', and follow each with the answer. For example:

• Did the person really die? (Answer: *Yes. He was executed by experts.*)

• Was the body stolen? (Answer: *No. The body was never produced.*)

• Did this person appear alive to anyone after his execution and disappearance from his grave? (Answer: *Yes, to well over 500 people on various occasions.*)

5 Say that the most reasonable explanation for this 'enigma' is: this person must have risen from the dead!

Application

1 Explain that the enigma you have just solved is not a made-up one like the ones in the game earlier. This enigma is actually the key to the Christian faith.

2 Many people through the centuries have asked many more questions than these about this amazing event. And they have ended up coming to the conclusion that Jesus Christ – the person buried in that grave in the cave – *did* come back to life from the dead, and he could only do this because he was none other than God himself.

39 UNBELIEVABLE!

aim

To help pupils consider that our knowledge of some events – which might otherwise have seemed unlikely – is reliably founded on eye-witness accounts.

You will need:

- *Either* an old, unwanted tie and a pair of scissors; *or* a tin of stewing steak with its label removed and a label from a can of dog food stuck in its place, a can opener and fork (if you use the latter, you will also need an assistant to help you in the assembly)
- 3 sets of 'T' (for 'true') and 'F' (for 'false') cards

Preparation

- Arrange with a teacher in advance to wear the old tie and take part in the tie-cutting exercise (see **Content** below).

Content

True or false?

1 Ask for three volunteers. Give them each a 'T' (for 'true') and an 'F' (for 'false') card. They must decide whether each of the following statements is true or false and then show the audience what they think by holding up the appropriate card.

- Julius Caesar's armies once invaded Britain. *(True)*
- Adolf Hitler's army drove, in a triumphant procession through the streets of London in 1943. *(False)*
- Prince Charles is the son of Queen Elizabeth II. *(True)*

2 At this stage, everyone should have all the answers correct. Make the point that this isn't too surprising, because all the statements so far describe well-known events. And even more important, there are reliable documents which prove that these things are true.

Say that all this makes the quiz too easy, so now you are going to try something else.

I don't believe it!

1 *Either*: take out a pair of sharp scissors and make your way to the member of staff wearing the old tie and, as arranged in

advance, cut the tie in half. Good acting is required as you feign nervousness for having done it, and as he pretends to be amazed and angry at the same time. Any over-the-top acting gives the game away!

Alternatively: introduce your assistant and say that at one time he or she was short of money and there wasn't much in the house to eat. One day, whilst feeding the dog, he or she just wondered what the dog food would taste like and was pleasantly surprised to find that it was delicious! Since then, from time to time, your assistant enjoys the occasional snack of dog food. Proceed to demonstrate this. Open the can. Your assistant takes a forkful and eats it to the astonishment and groans of the audience!

2 Make the point that if they were to go home after school and tell their families that someone came into school today and cut a teacher's tie in half (or ate dog food), people would be likely to say they were imagining it or telling lies. Point out that they could say that they saw it with their own eyes and that it wasn't just one person who saw it, there were ... (fill in however many) in the assembly!

3 After Jesus rose from the dead, well over 500 people were eye-witnesses to the fact that he was alive again, and some of them faithfully recorded their amazing experiences which convinced them that these things really did happen.

Telling huge lies like the one about Adolf Hitler marching through London is always likely to catch you out, because people can say, 'Hang on a minute, I was there!' You can't get away with it!

Application

1 Christians today don't base their faith on wishful thinking or legends. They rely on the evidence of eye-witness accounts, just as we do for any historical event.

2 And the extra significance of Easter for Christians is that the resurrection proves Jesus to be just who he said he was – God, in human form, with power over death and the promise of life beyond.

3 Conclude with this challenge to pupils: the next time they see a tin of dog food (or are tempted to cut someone's tie in half), let it remind them of another seemingly outrageous event that actually happened!

WORK EXPERIENCE

40 WORK, WORK, WORK!

Note: This assembly is for use in preparation for work experience and is intended for use with older pupils.

aim

To help pupils examine the nature of work; and to think about Jesus' attitude to work.

Bible base

Matthew 20:1-16
– the workers in the vineyard.

You will need:

*   Items for task assignments: potatoes and peeler; dirty shoes, polish and brushes; pencils and sharpener; 26 cards showing the different letters of the alphabet
*   A hat containing 4 cards showing assignments
*   4 small prizes (eg chocolate bars)
*   An OHP and 3 acetates showing:
    OHP 1 – a 'graffiti board' style list of issues which are part of the world of work (see **Content** below)
    OHP 2 – a picture of a famous person (eg well-known sports or music celebrity)
    OHP 3 – a picture of Mother Teresa
*   Some music for timing the work activity (see **Content** below)

Content

Introduction
1 Tell pupils that as it's the time of year for 'work experience', you are going to give them some practice.
2 Ask for four volunteers and give them each one of the following tasks together with the necessary equipment:
*   peel three potatoes;

- clean and polish a pair of shoes;
- sharpen a dozen pencils;
- sort the twenty-six cards into alphabetical order.

3 Having told everyone what the four jobs are, assign the four volunteers their tasks by asking them to pull a card out of a hat. (Comment that you are sure that more care was taken in their real work placements!)

4 Play some music (it could be on the theme of work, or some 'busy' music like *The Flight of the Bumble-bee* by Rimsky-Korsakov), while they do their jobs. After one minute, see how they've got on.

5 Give the volunteers a round of applause and a small reward. You could say something like, 'Don't expect anything like that on work experience!'

Why work?

1 Ask some rhetorical questions about the nature of work. For example:

- Do we work only for what we can get out of it ourselves?
- Does it matter whether we work willingly or begrudgingly, as long as the job gets done?
- What is 'work', anyway? Is what we do in school 'work'? Or is 'work' only a 'proper job' for which you get paid? What about 'working' in the garden or the house all day? Is that work? Or leisure?

2 Say to your audience that as they are preparing for the world of work, it's worth remembering some of the similarities, as well as the differences, between school and work. **Display OHP 1** (or large piece of card) showing some of the different issues involved in work which may or may not be part of their working life at school or in 'a job'. You could include: punctuality, hours, holidays, working day, rules, law, discipline, contract, clothing, illness, wages, pay.

You might talk about some of these or just leave them on display whilst you make the general point that the wonderful stress-free, hassle-free, world of work out there doesn't exist! And probably, the things you dislike about school will be present, in some form, at work.

3 Display OHP 2 (eg a top sports person, a super-model or filmstar). Then **display OHP 3** – the picture of Mother Teresa. Ask some questions like:

- Whose job is the most important?
- Whose job is the best paid?
- Are there other criteria we need to consider?

4 Talk about the fact that even though they won't be paid for the work they do on work experience, that doesn't mean they are not important, or that the work they do next week doesn't count.

Say that some people on work experience have made a real difference to their place of work: because of the kind of person they are; the atmosphere they've helped to create. And, as a result, they've made a lasting impression on their workmates.

5 Tell this story: There was a man who had a big job which had to be done in one day. So, he hired some men to do it for a fixed daily rate. Half-way through the day, he realised that the job wasn't going to be completed on time. So he took on some more men at the same rate. In the early evening, he took on some more to make sure everything was finished and packed away. All the men got the same pay. Some of them didn't like it, but the boss told them that they'd all got what was agreed at the time they were taken on.

6 Explain that Jesus told this story (see Matthew 20:1-16) – not to make out a case for everyone to be paid the same – but to show that everyone was equally important in getting the job done on time. They all had a part to play, however small it seemed.

Application

1 Say that you are sure they will all work very hard during work experience, and for no apparent reward.

2 Tell pupils that Jesus was a worker for many years. He knew what it was like to get dirt in his fingernails and to trade and bargain for the best deals. But Jesus said something very ironic about his work. He said that the most important thing he had come to do was to serve others and eventually die for them, not to gain a reward for himself, but for the greatest free reward ever for others; the best 'bonus' any boss could give to anyone, no matter how deserving – the gift of eternal life ... heaven.

FURTHER RESOURCES AND ADDRESSES

More useful books

- *52 Ideas for Secondary School Classroom Assemblies,* Janet King, Monarch.
- *More Great Ideas for Secondary Classroom Assemblies,* Janet King, Monarch.
- *Assembly Line, Andrew Smith,* CPAS: teaching the Bible in assemblies (11s-14s).
- *Leading Worship in Schools,* Janet King, Monarch: a practical guide for visitors to schools.
- *The Schools Work Handbook,* Emlyn Williams, Scripture Union: intended to help those who are working in schools to think through what they do there and to be more effective in their minisry.
- *Support Your Local School,* Schools Ministry Network: available from the address given below.

Audio visual resources

Scripture Union produce a wide range of audio cassettes and videos suitable for use in schools. For further details, contact Scripture Union Sound and Vision Unit, 207-209 Queensway, Bletchley, Milton Keynes, Buckinghashire, MK2 2EB; telephone (01908) 856000, fax (01908) 856111.

Addresses

Scripture Union provides support and training for those involved in schools work and can be contacted at:

- Scripture Union in Schools (England and Wales), 207-209 Queensway, Bletchley, Milton Keynes, Buckinghamshire, MK2 2EB;
  telephone (01908) 856000, fax (01908) 865111.
- Scripture Union (Scotland), 9 Canal Street, Glasgow, G4 0AB.
- Scripture Union (Northern Ireland), 157 Alberbridge Road, Belfast, BT5 4PS.
- Scripture Union (Republic of Ireland), 87 Lower Georges Street, Dun Laoghaire, Co. Dublin.

Schools Ministry Network links Christian schools workers through regular mailings and conferences. It can also provide addresses of organisations working in schools in your area. Schools Ministry Network can be contacted at: Schools Ministry Network, 207-209 Queensway, Bletchley, Milton Keynes, Buckinghamshire, MK2 2EB; telephone (01908) 856000, fax (01908) 856111.

Stapleford House Education Centre (Association of Christian Teachers) provides a variety of resources for Christian teachers including excellent assembly materials. The centre also runs courses throughout the year, some of which are especially relevant to those involved in schools work as visitors. For further details write to: Stapleford House Education Centre, Wesley Place, Stapleford, Nottingham NG9 8DP; telephone (0115) 939 6270.

Christian Publicity Organisation produces a wide range of leaflets which could be useful for assemblies (eg. the *Hey!* leaflet and *10 reasons why I never wash*). Write to: CPO, Garcia Estate, Canterbury Road, Worthing, W. Sussex. BN13 1BW; telephone (01903) 264556.